ALPHABET BOOK FOR KIDS

Woo! Jr
kids activities

Copyright © 2020, Woo! Jr. Kids Activities, LLC

Woo! Jr. Kids Activities & Wendybird Press Founder: Wendy Piersall
Art Director: Lilia Garvin
Production Designer: Ethan Piersall
Cover Illustration: Michael Koch | Sleeping Troll Studios www.sleepingtroll.com
Editing & Proofreading: Lori Acosta

Published by:
Wendybird Press
226 W. Judd
Woodstock IL, 60098
www.wendybirdpress.com

ISBN-13: 978-1732958999
ISBN-10: 1732958998

wendybird
press

How to Use This Book

Each letter has a bubble letter coloring page, a unique word coloring page, a hidden picture puzzle, a maze, and a word & letter tracing activity!

In Hidden Pictures: find the shapes listed in the shape answer key inside the puzzle. You can color the right shapes in with pencil or crayon, or circle them.

Solve the mazes by going from one star to the other!

Use the letter & word tracing pages for tracing practice!

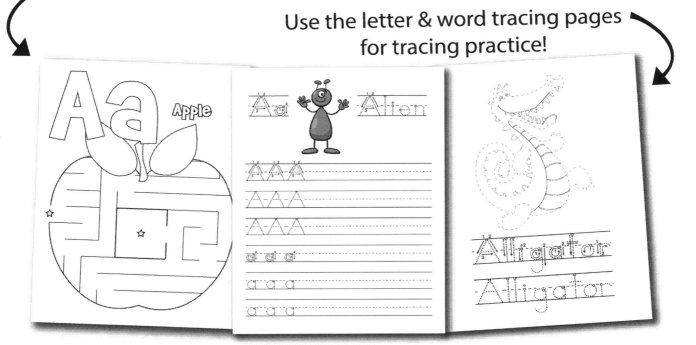

Free Download!

Like this book?

Join our VIP mailing list and get a _FREE_ 70 page printable PDF _Holiday Activity Book for Kids_! It includes crosswords, word searches, picture matching, and coloring activities for ages 4-10!

Holidays include:
Martin Luther King Jr. Day
Valentine's Day
St. Patrick's Day
Easter
Earth Day
4th of July
Halloween
Thanksgiving
Hanukkah
Christmas

Get Started here:

www.woojr.com/free-book

Alligator

ANCHOR

Astronaut

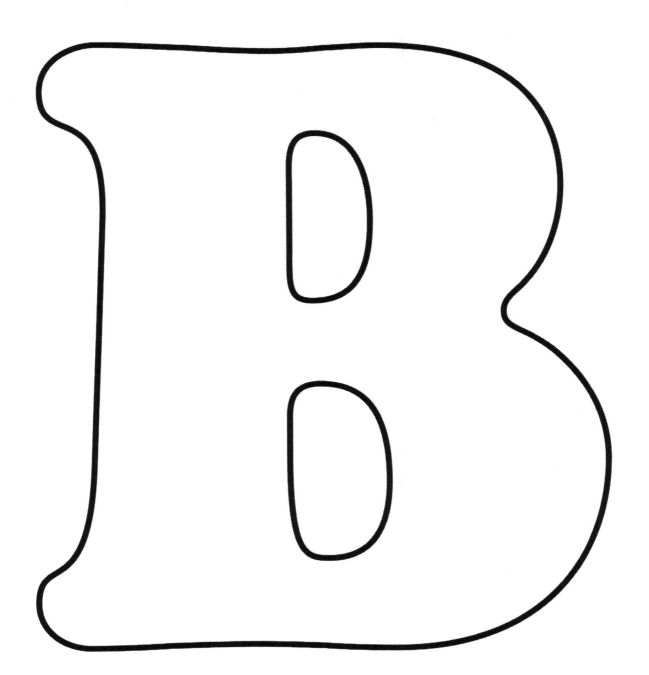

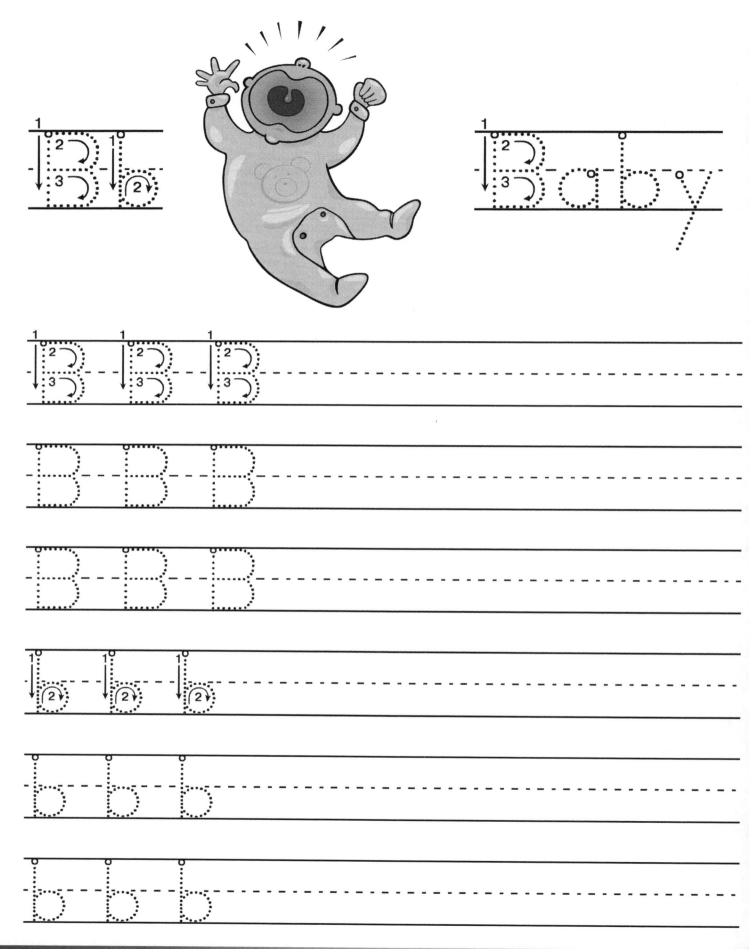

Baby

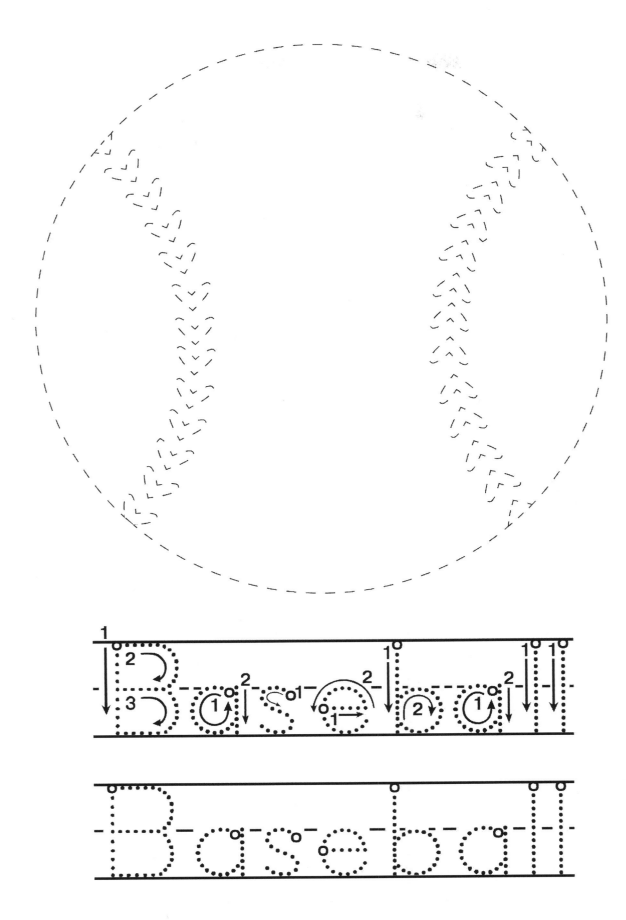

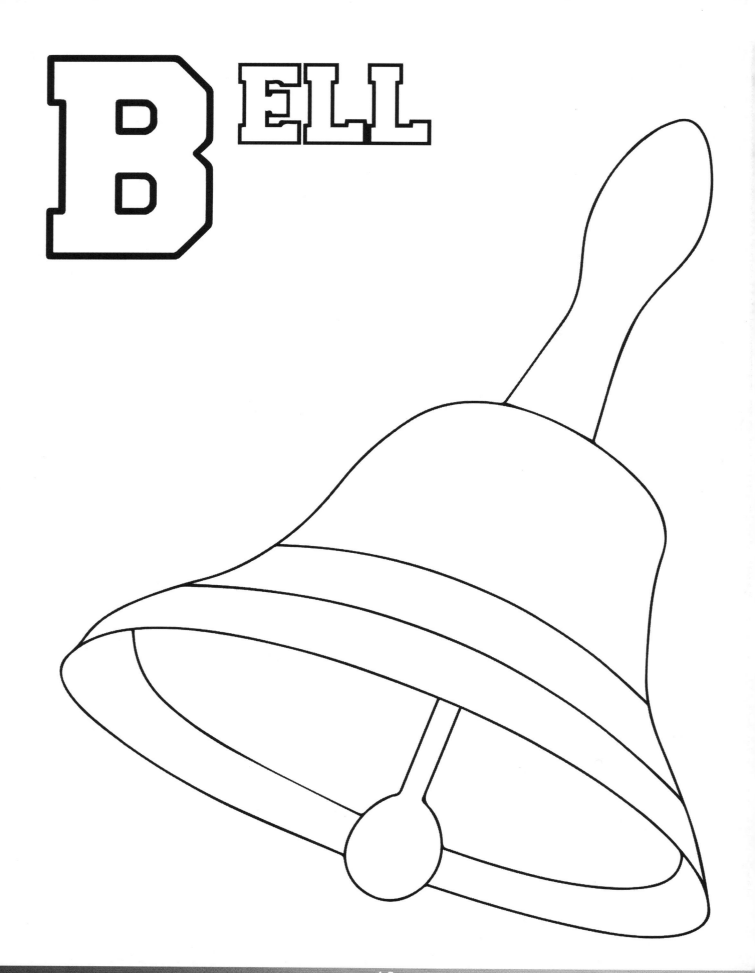

Beetle

Basketball

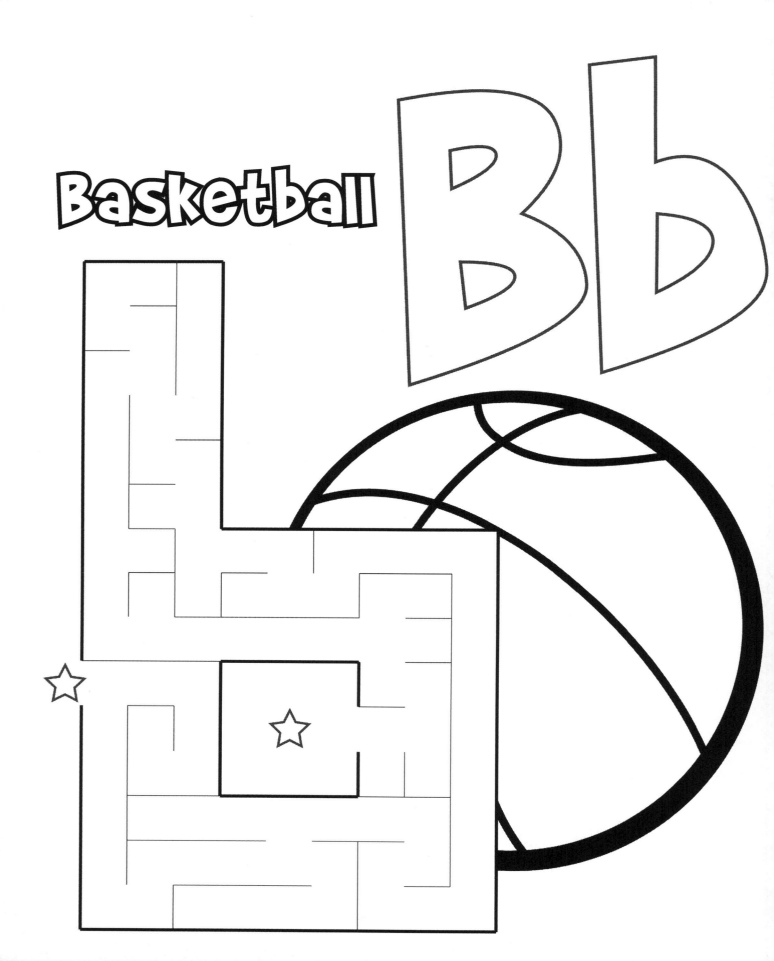

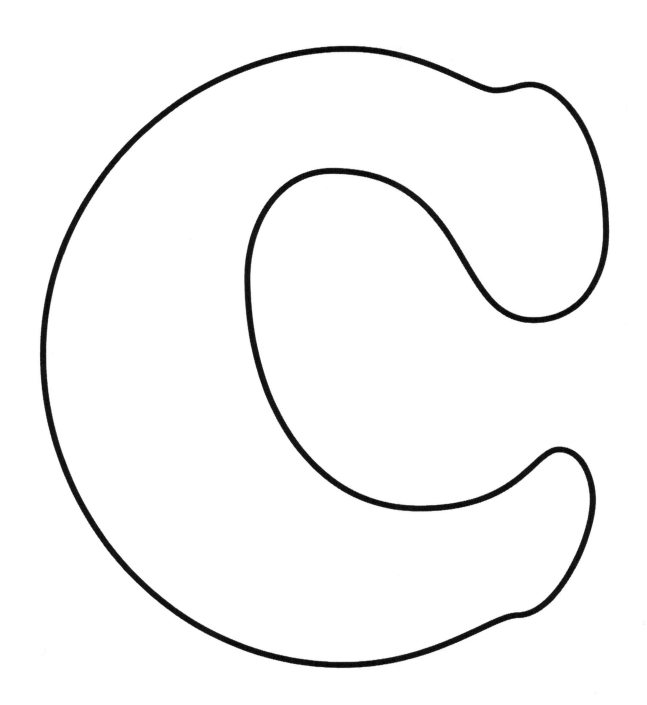

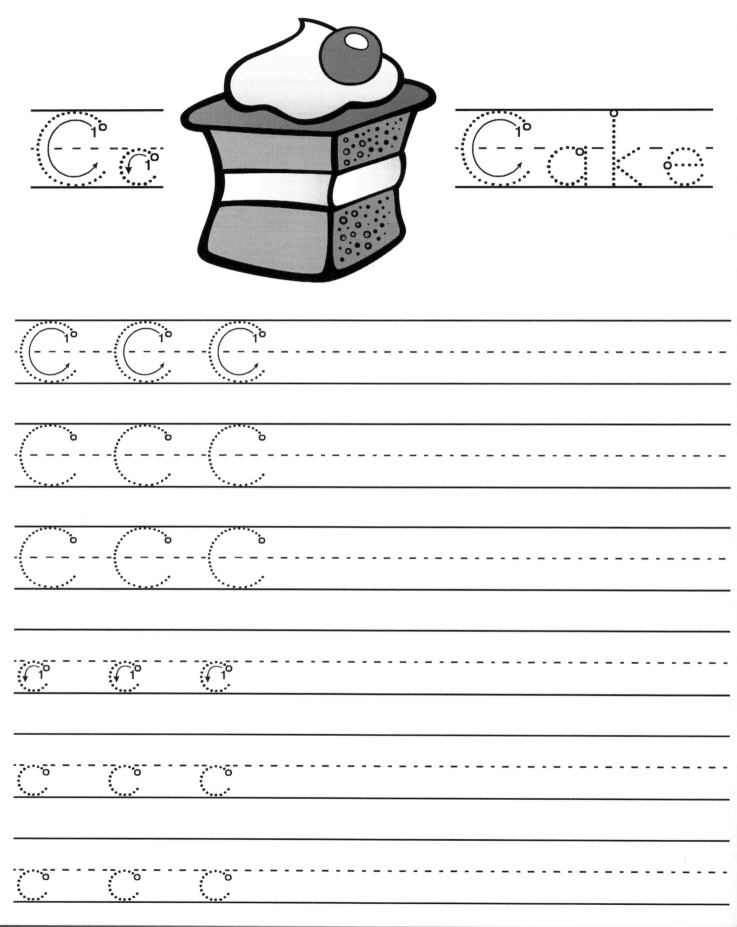

CAMERA

Camping

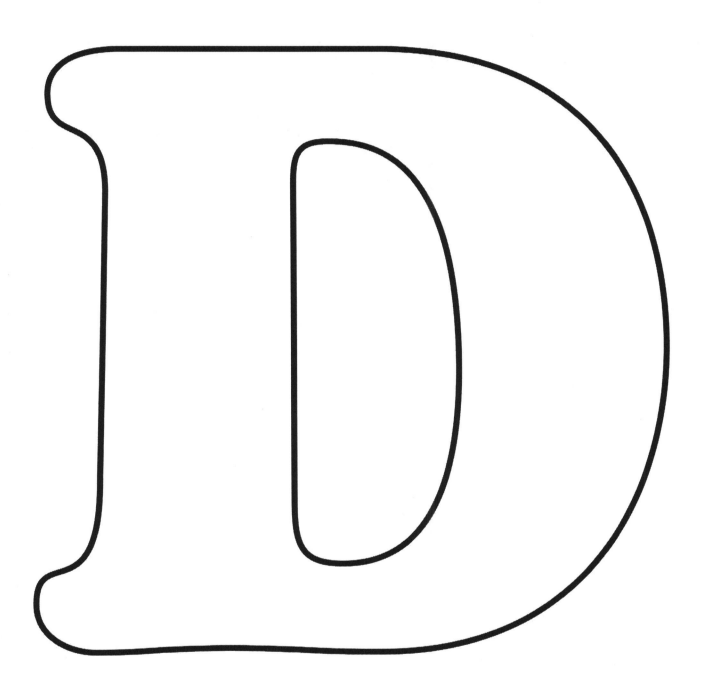

Donut

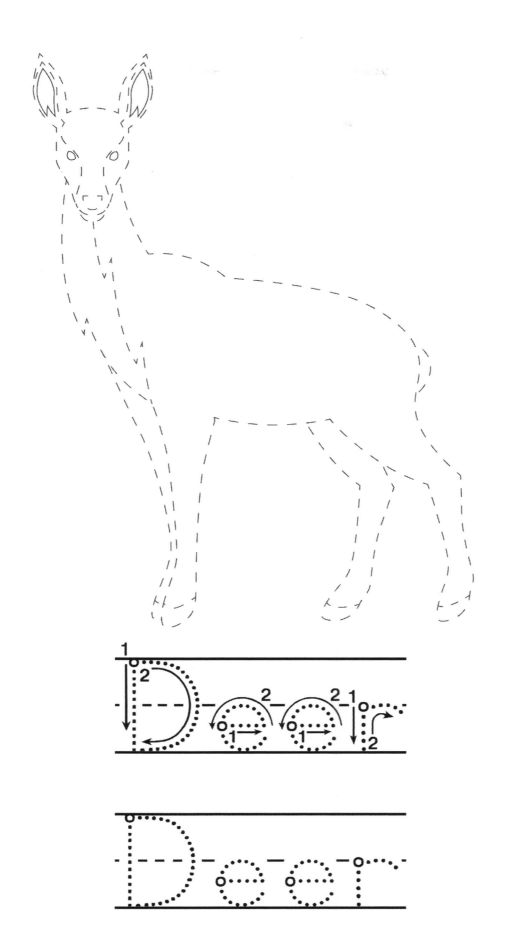

Deer

DINOSAUR

Dragon

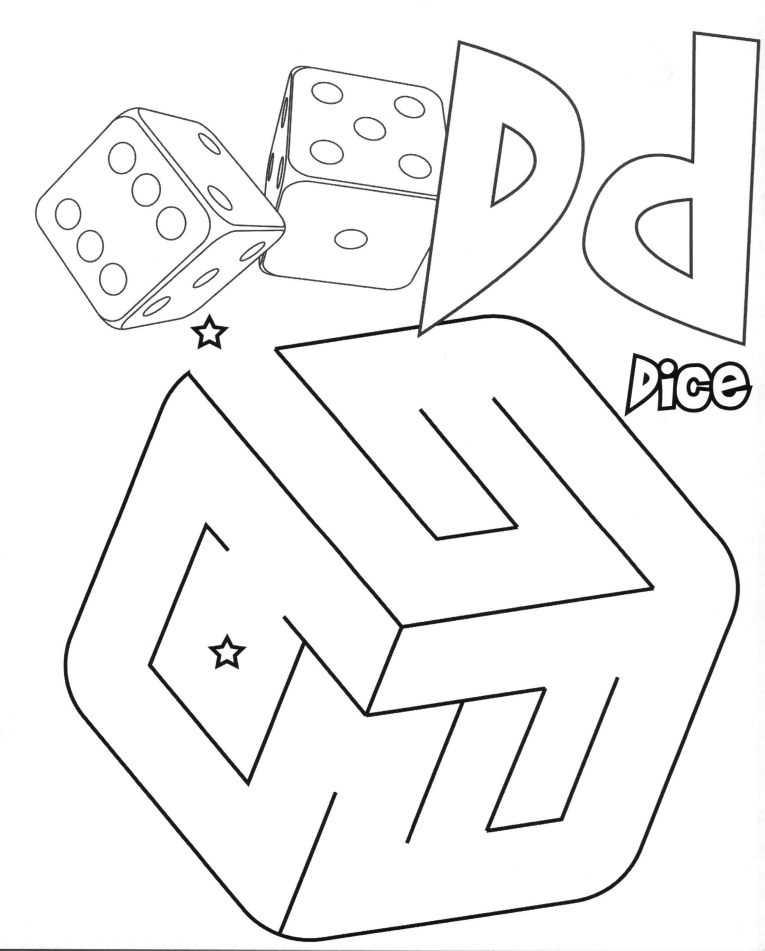

Dice

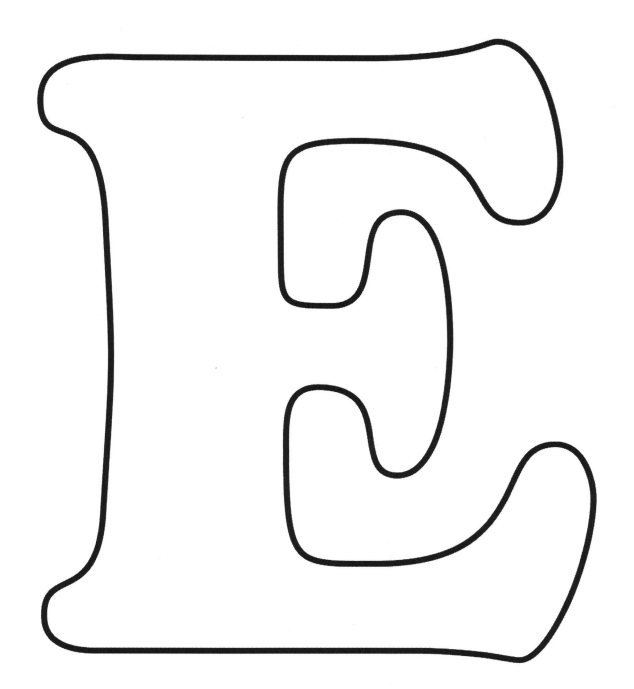

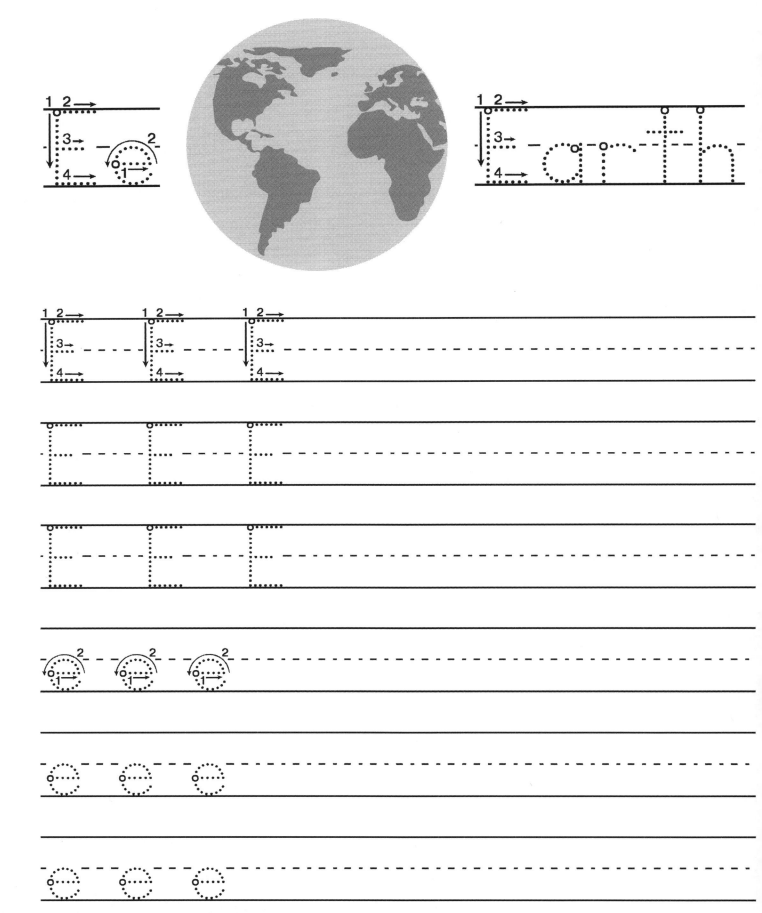

ELEPHANT

Eating

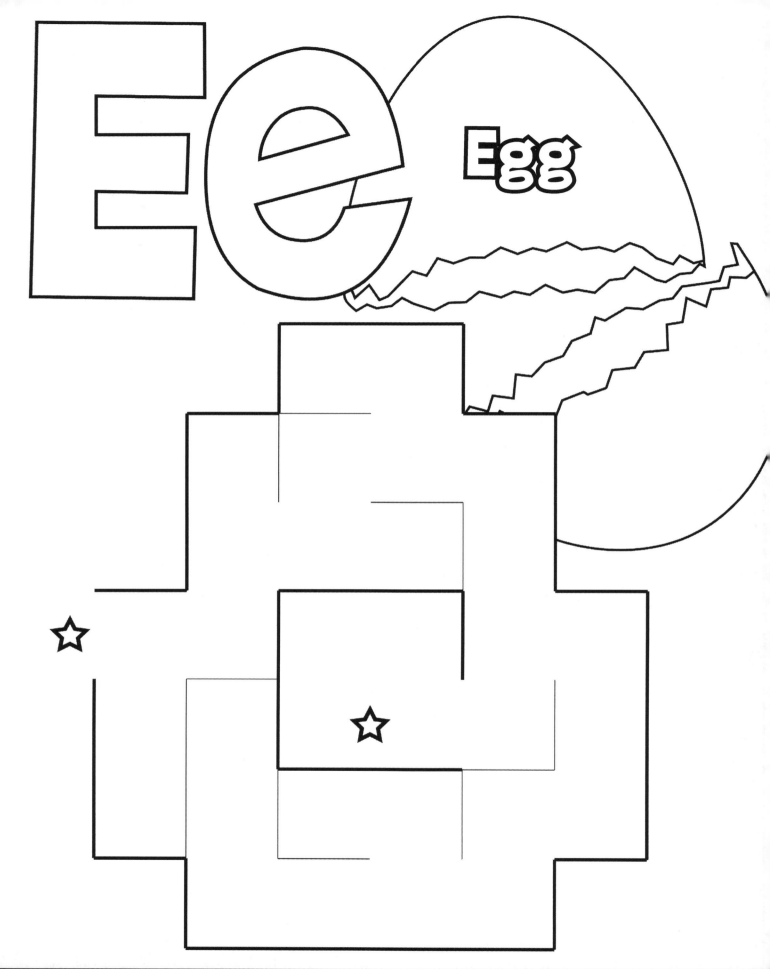

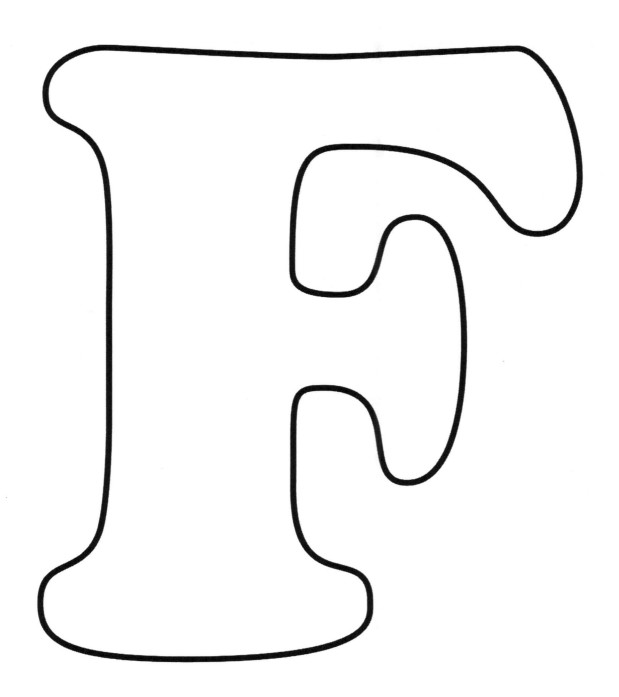

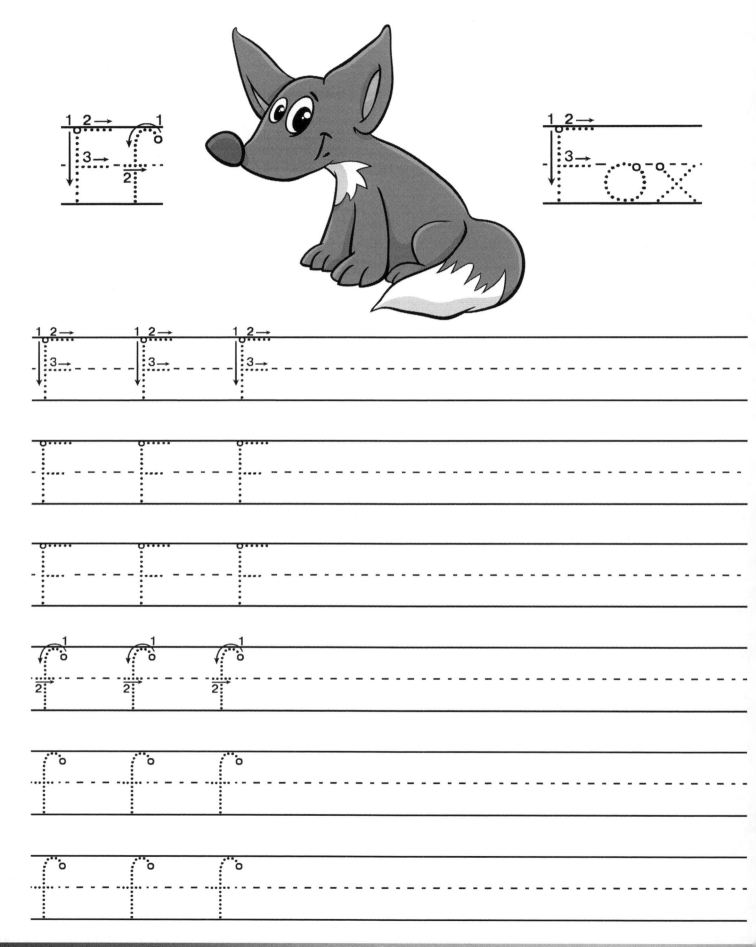

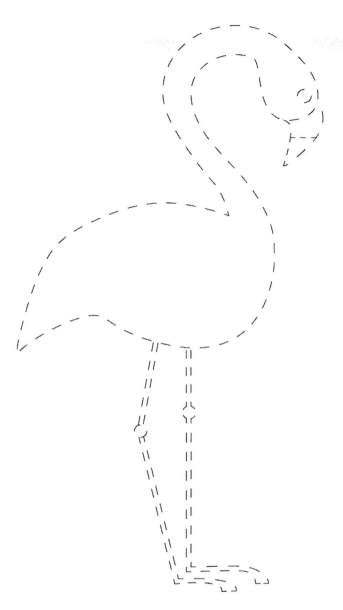

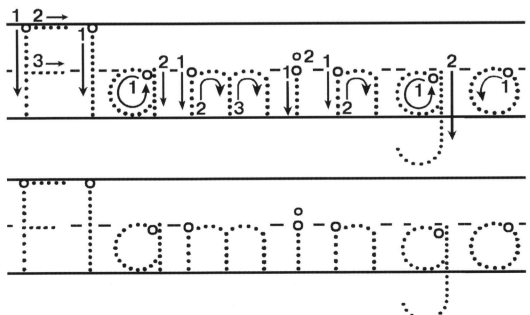

FIREWORKS

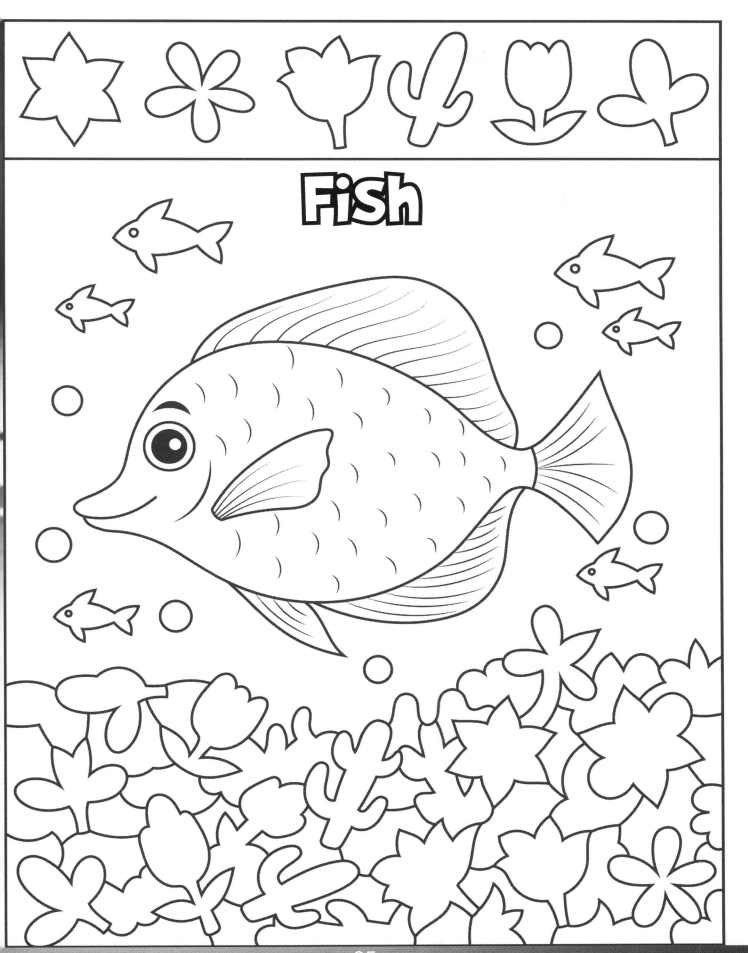

Fish

Frog

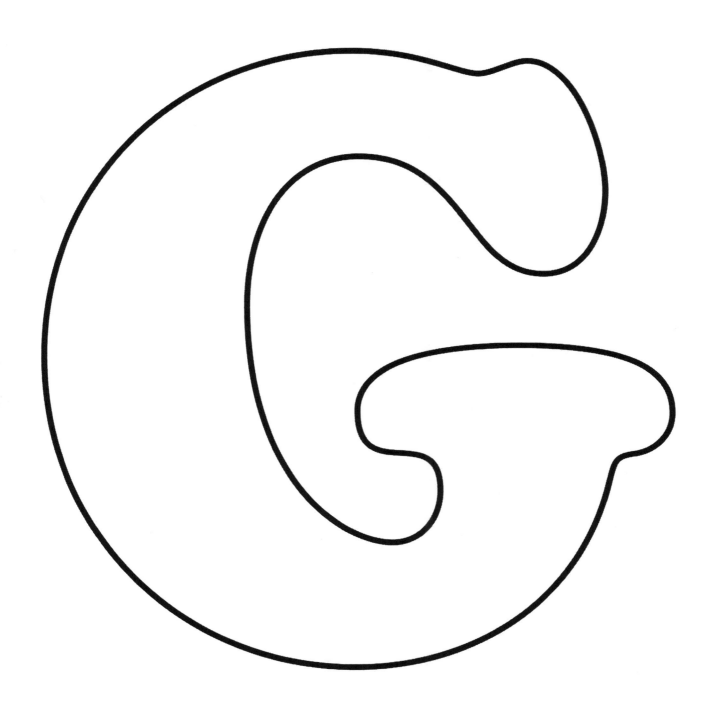

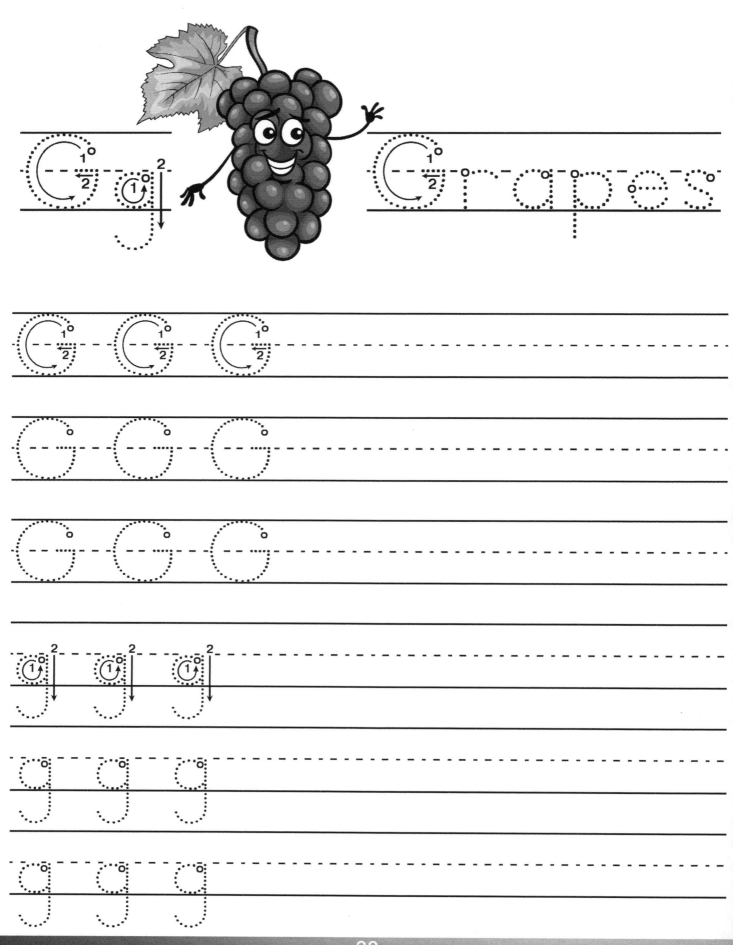

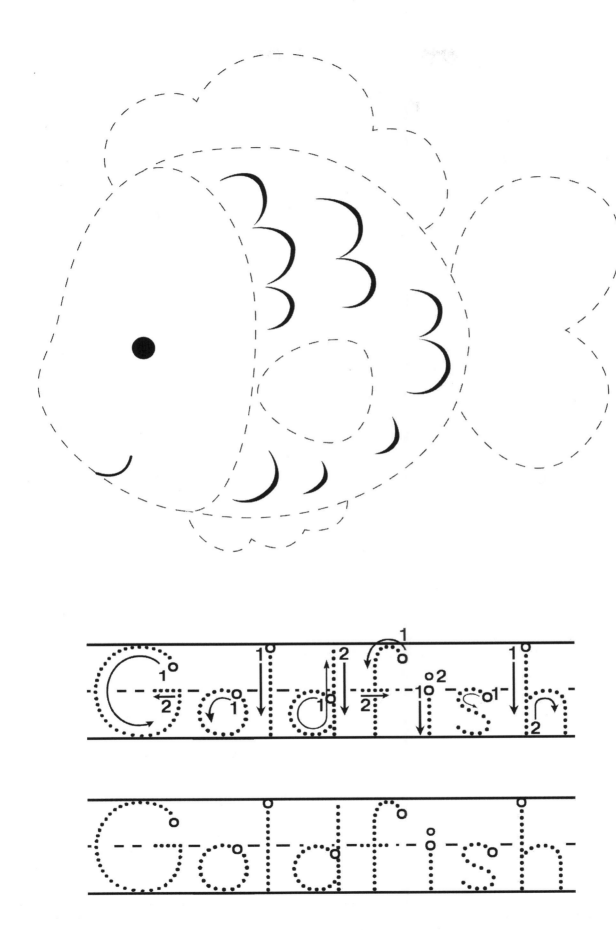

Groundhog

Goat

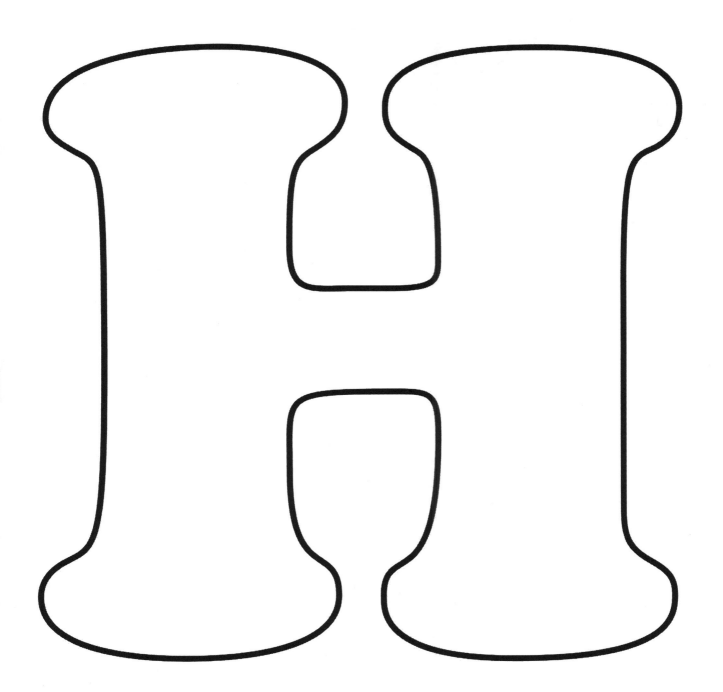

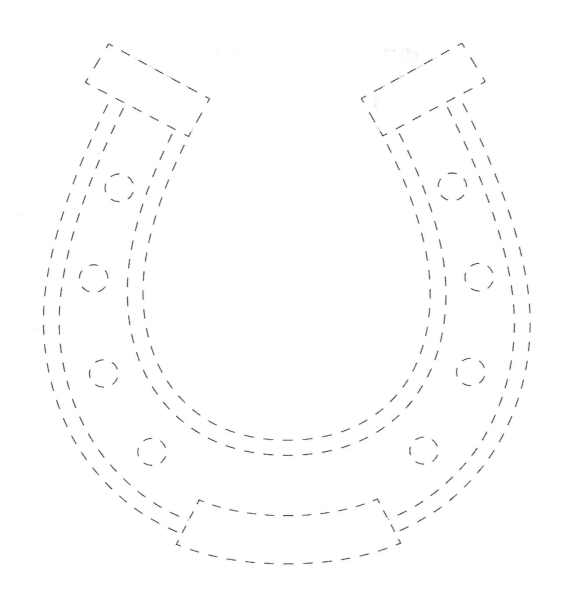

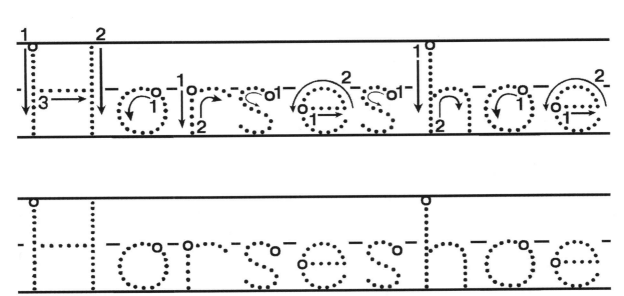

Hedgehog

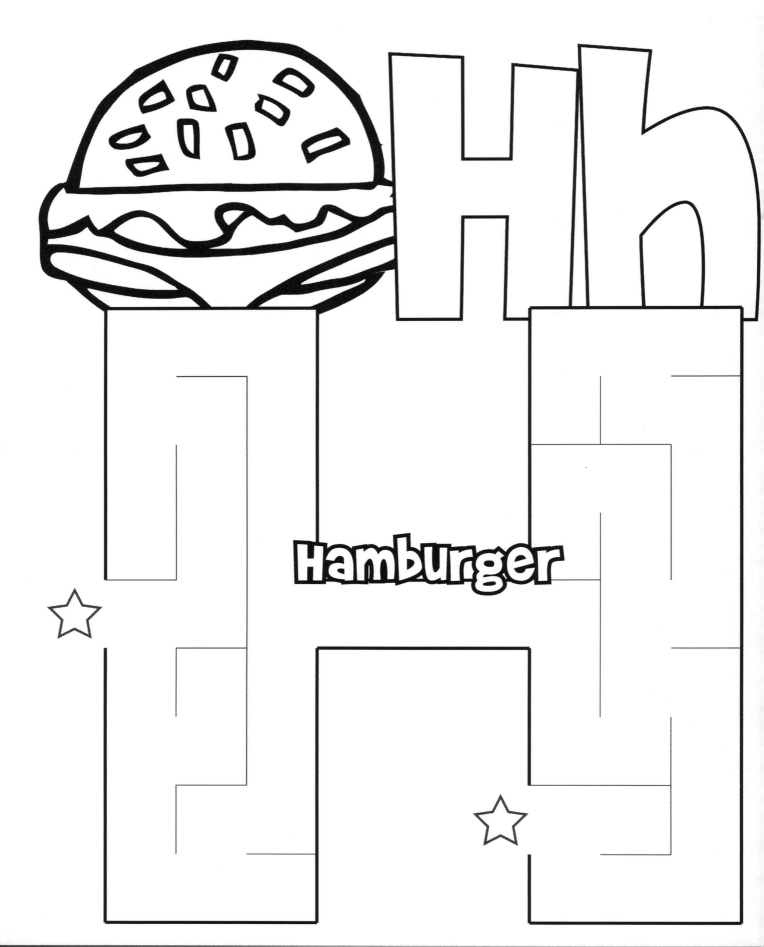

Hamburger

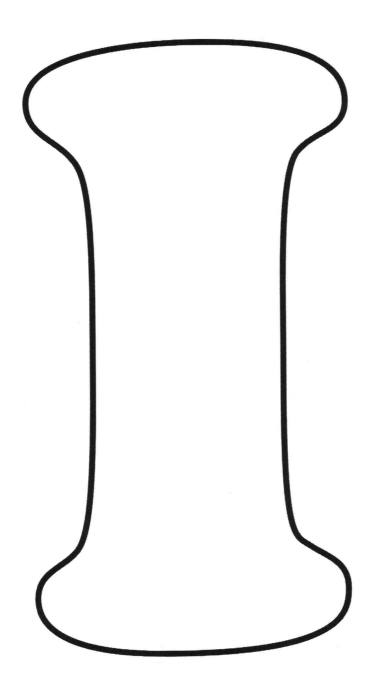

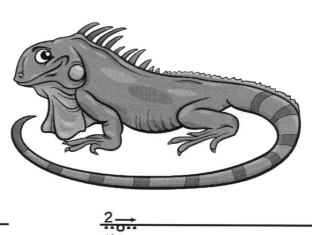

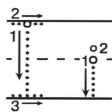

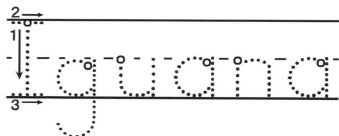

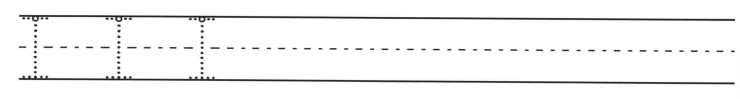

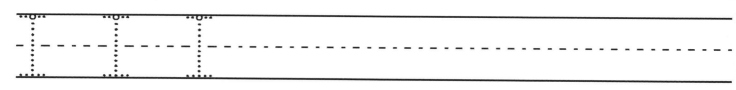

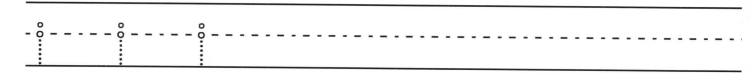

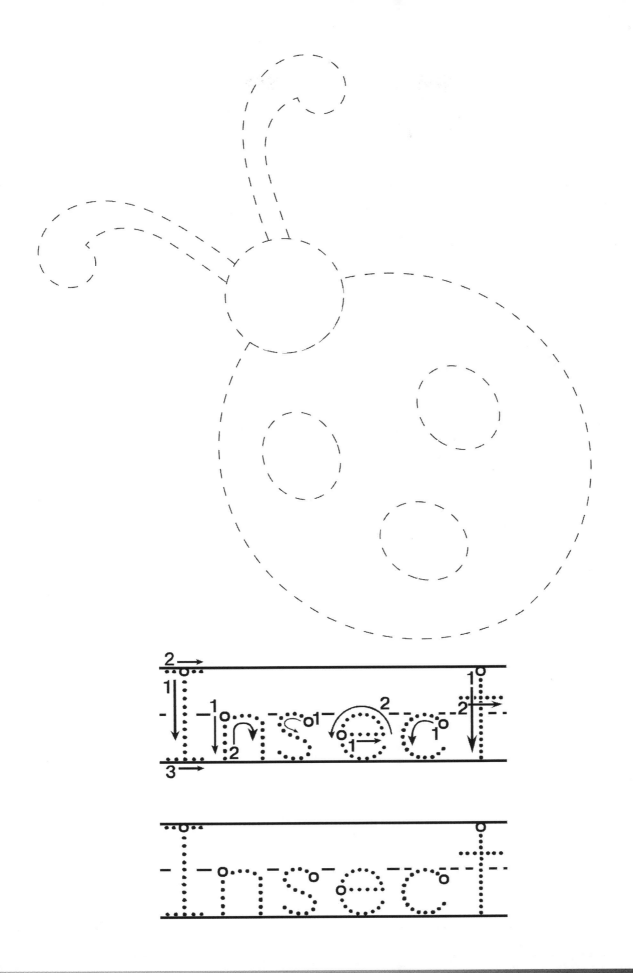

ICE CREAM

Instrument

Ii Igloo

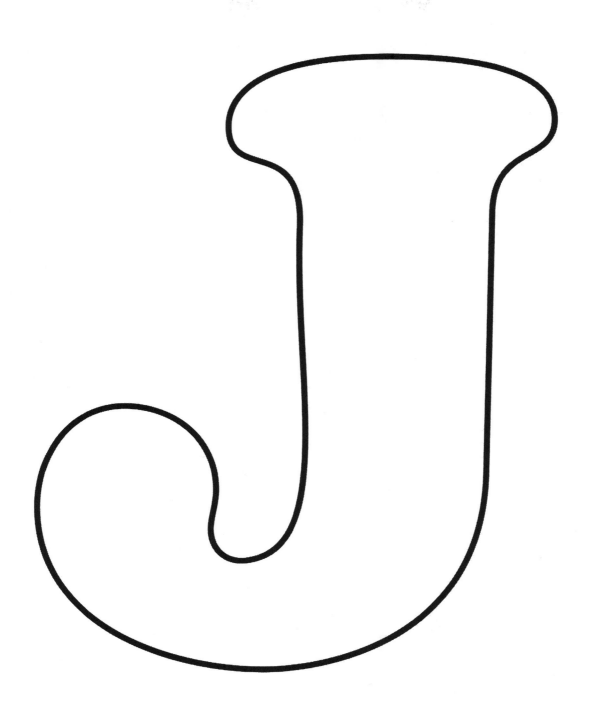

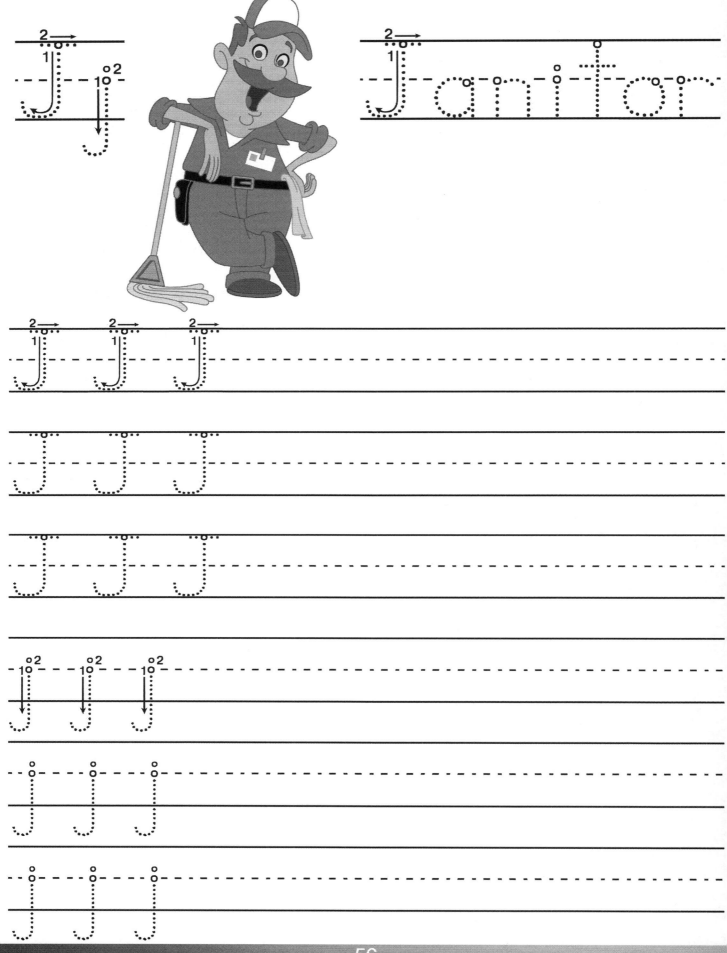

J a n i t o r

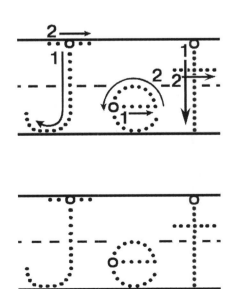

JELLYFISH

Jack-o-lantern

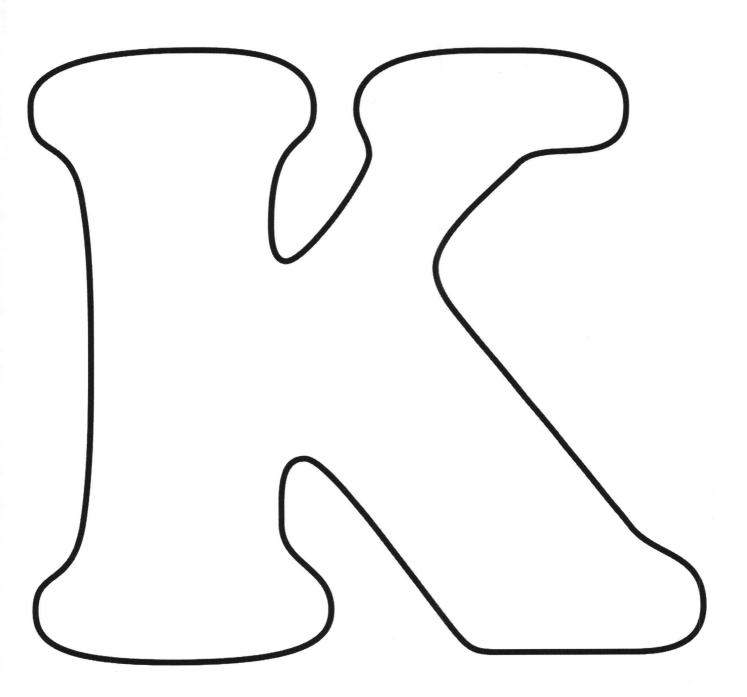

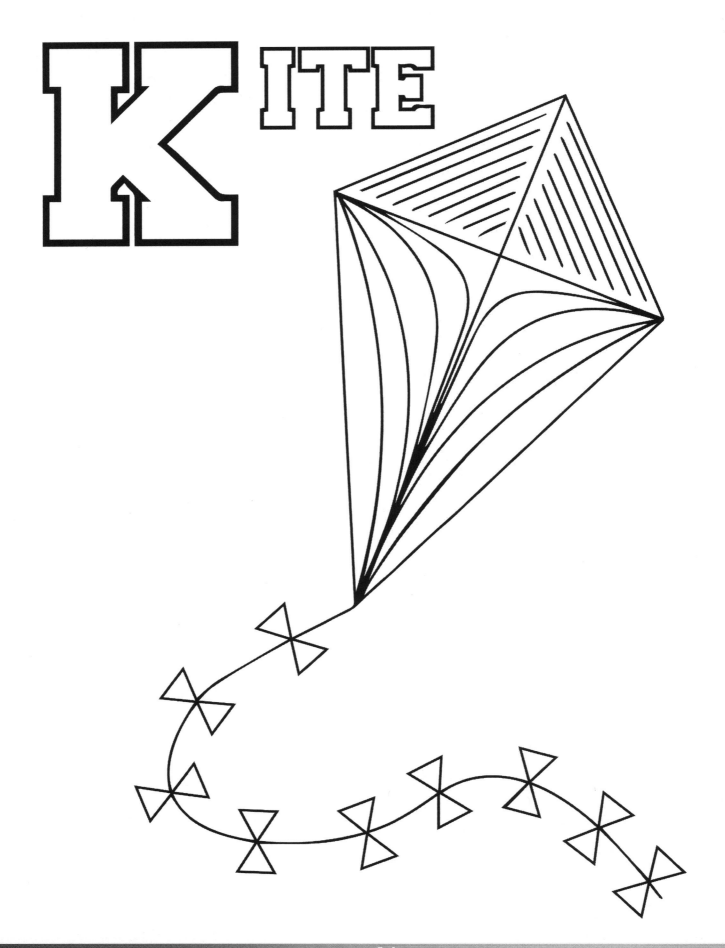

Kitten

Kk kettle

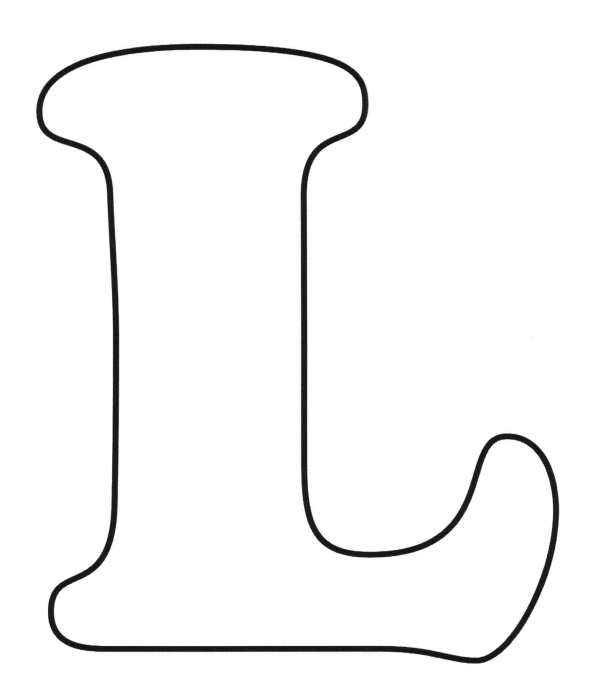

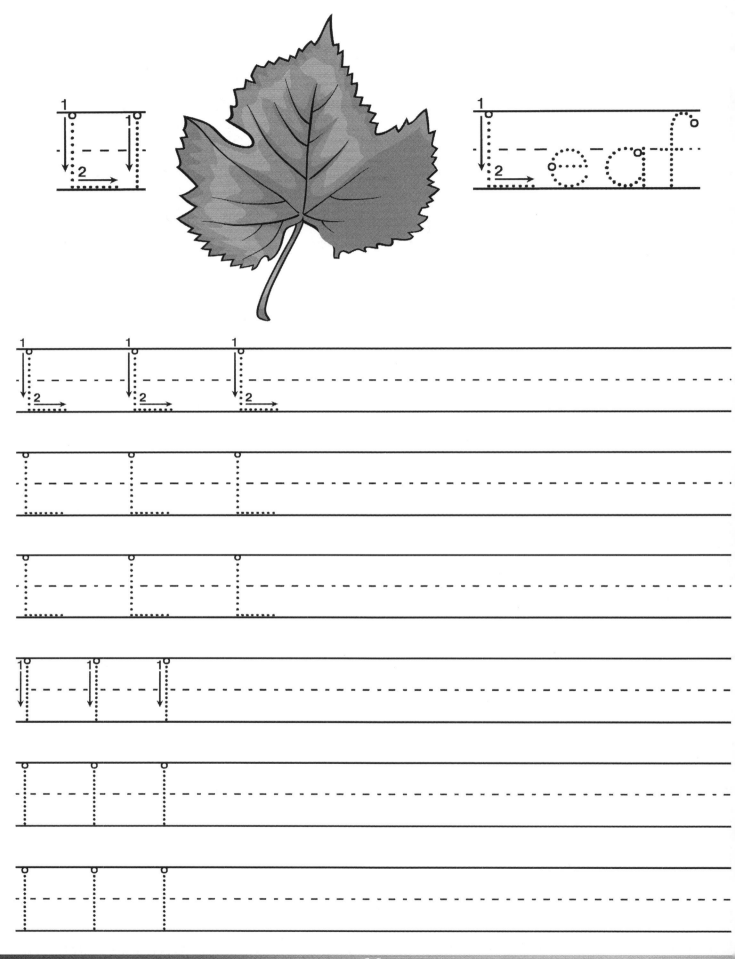

LOBSTER

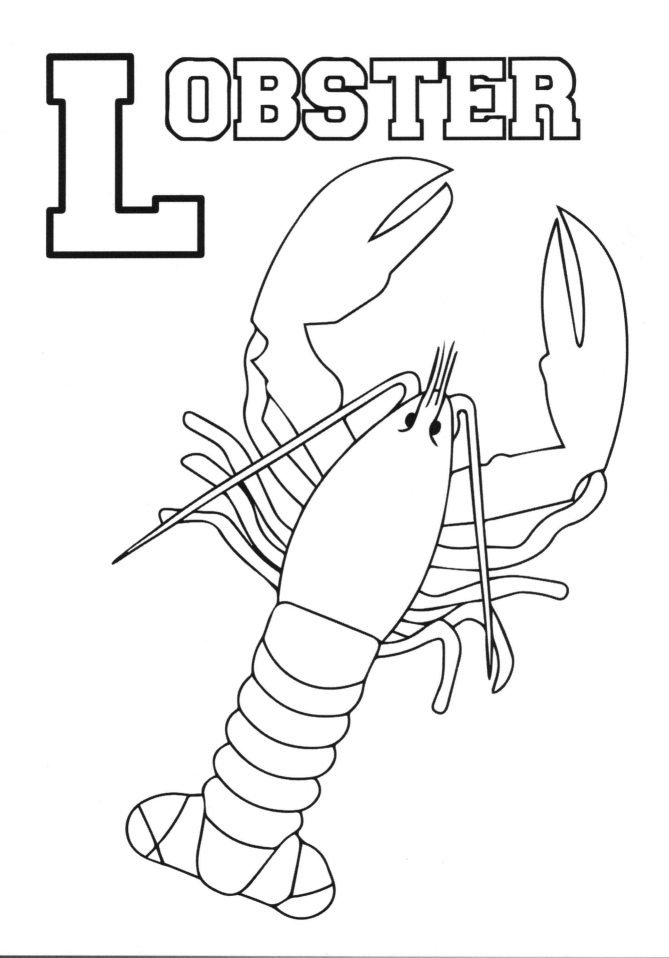

Llama

Lemon

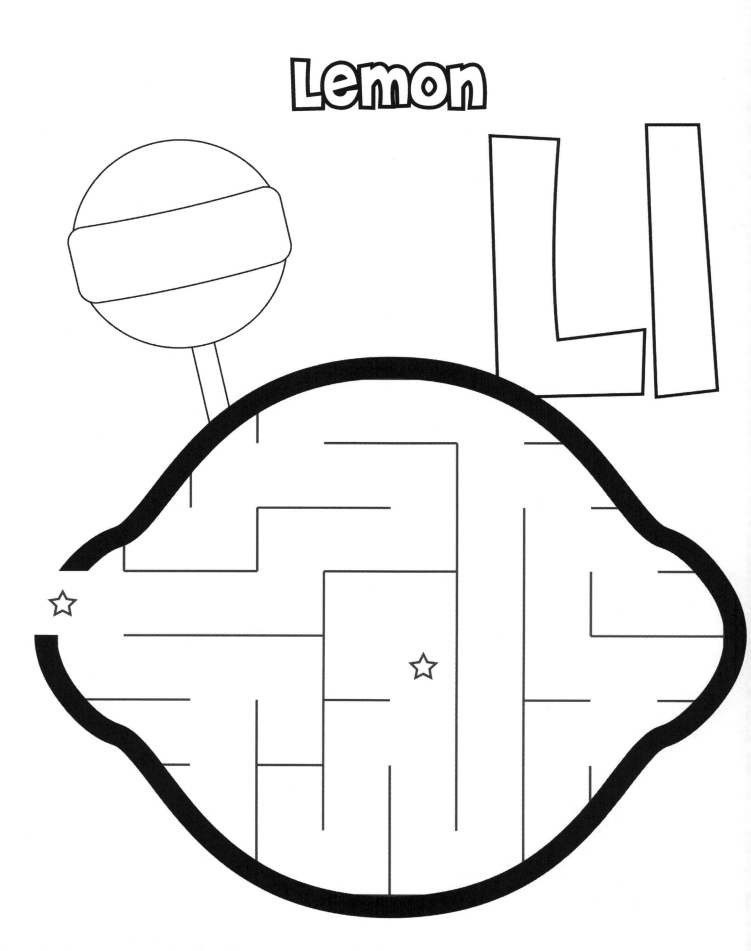

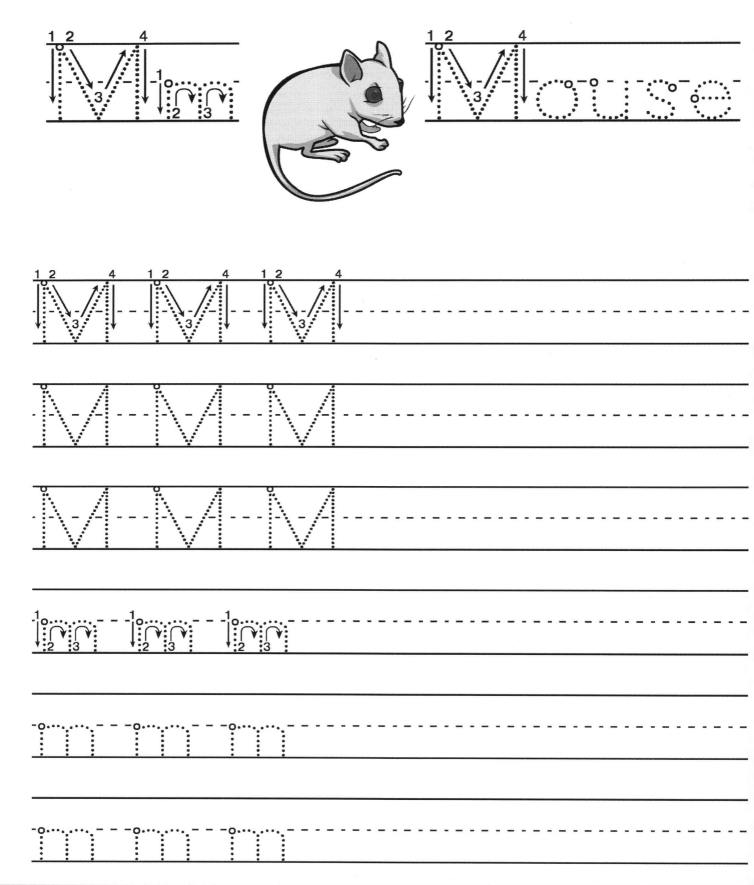

Mess

Moth

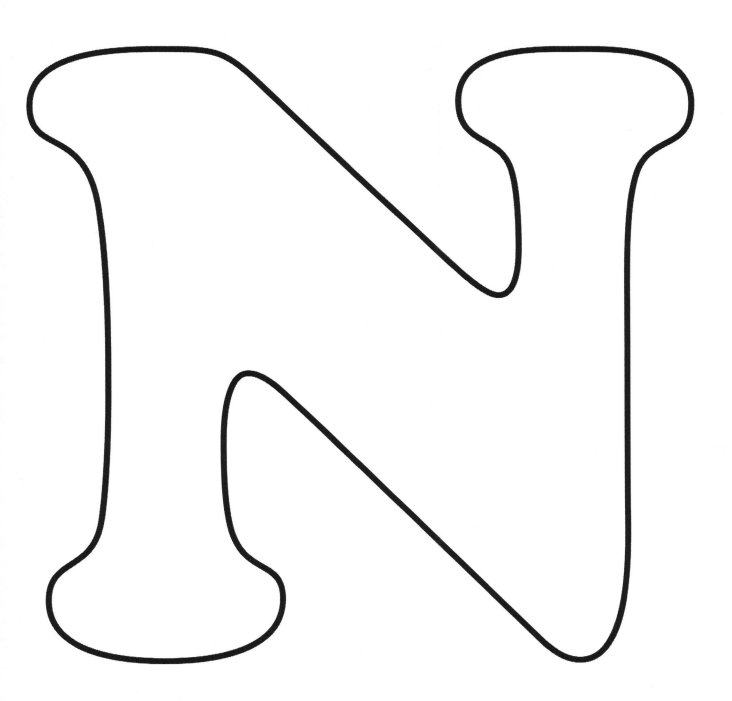

Nurse

NARWHAL

Necks

Nest

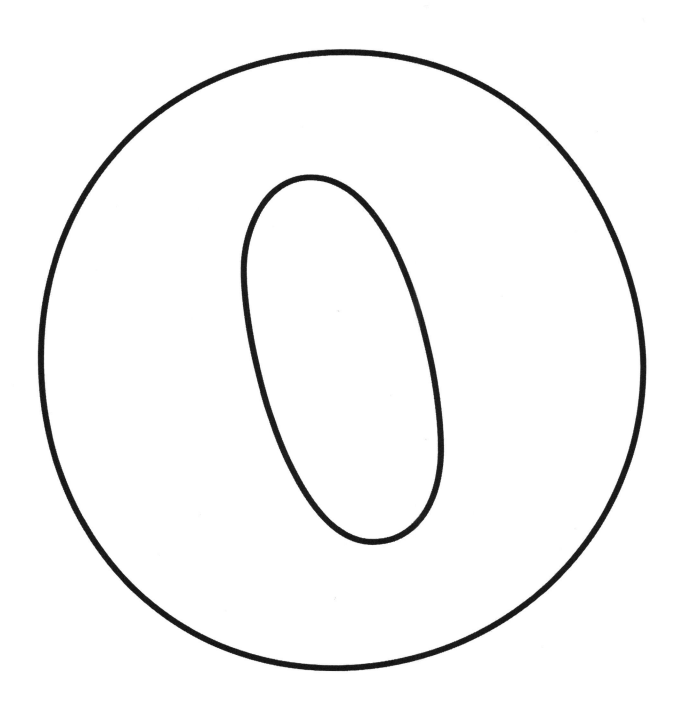

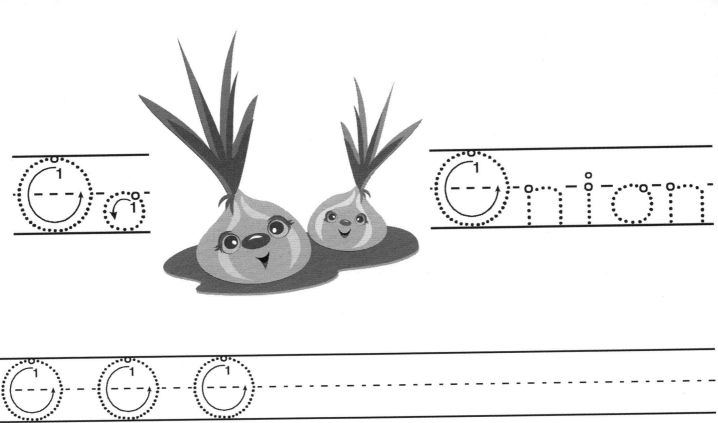

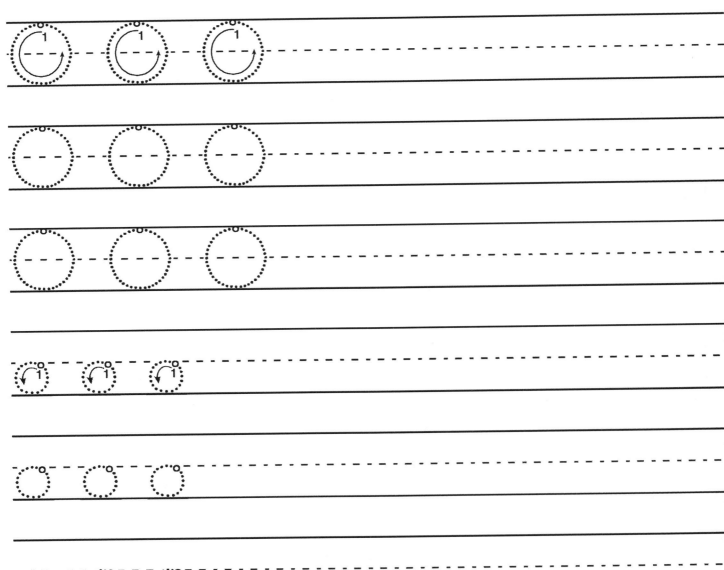

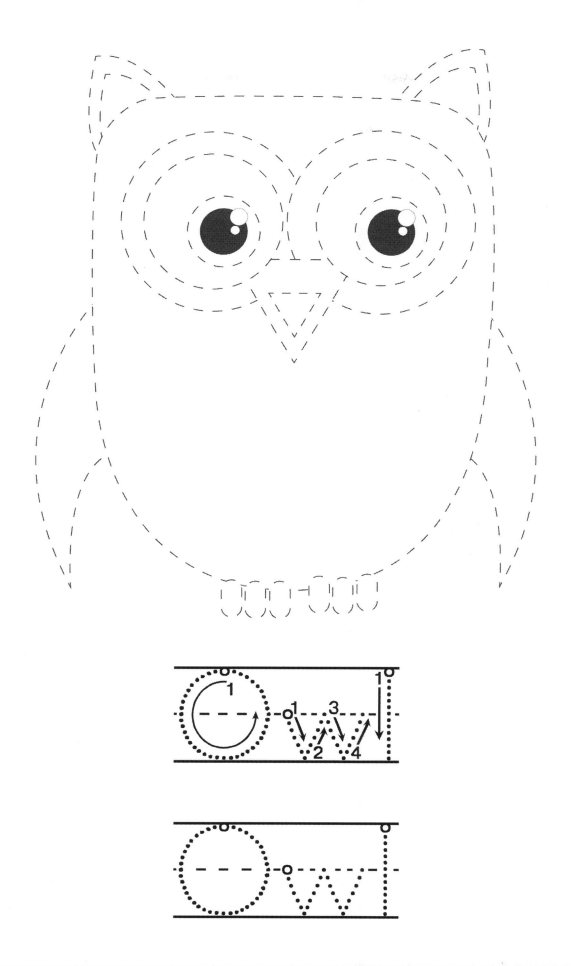

OCTOPUS

Ostrich

Orange

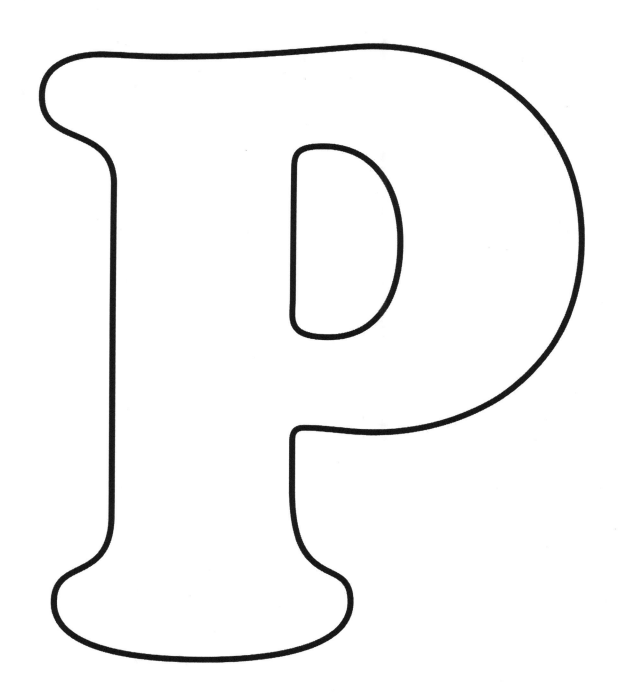

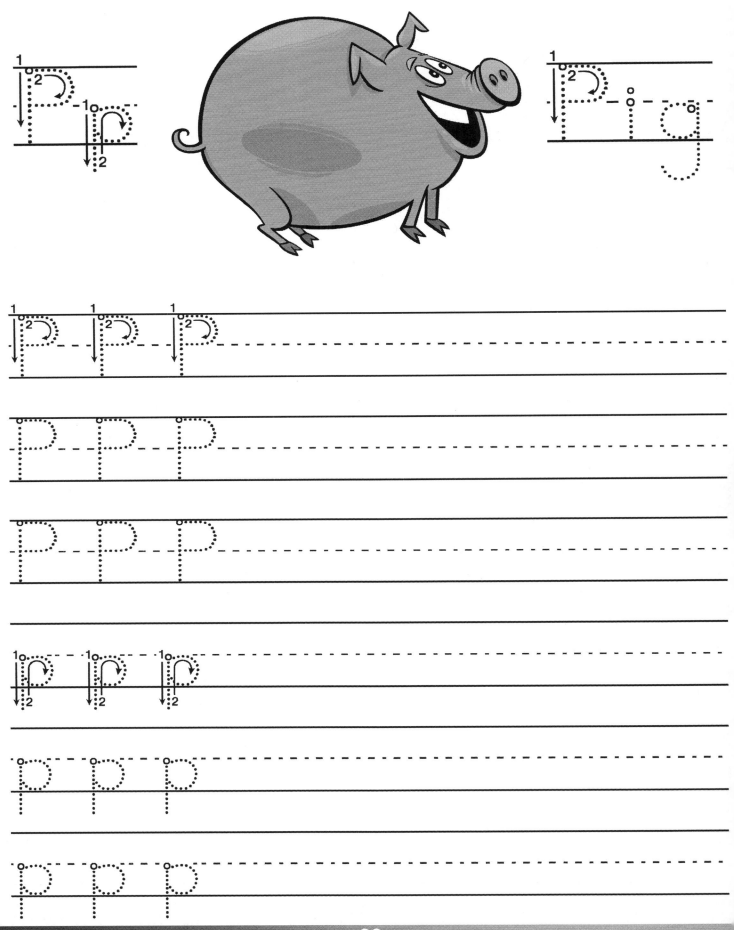

PINEAPPLE

Pool

Parrot

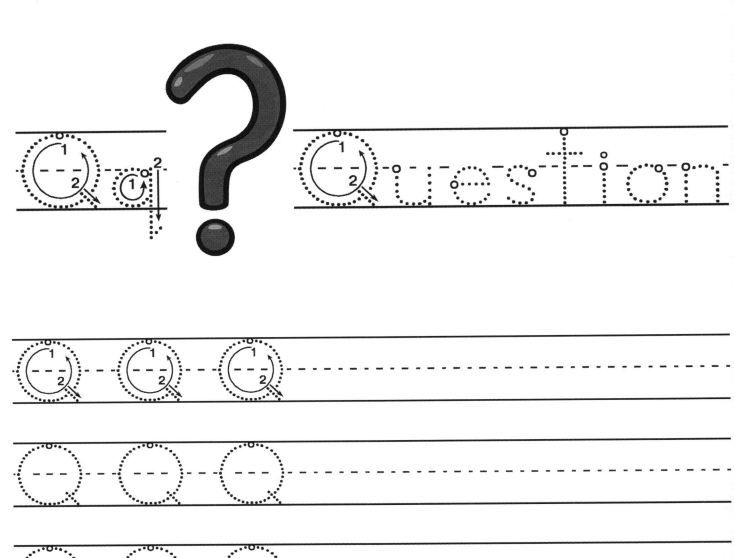

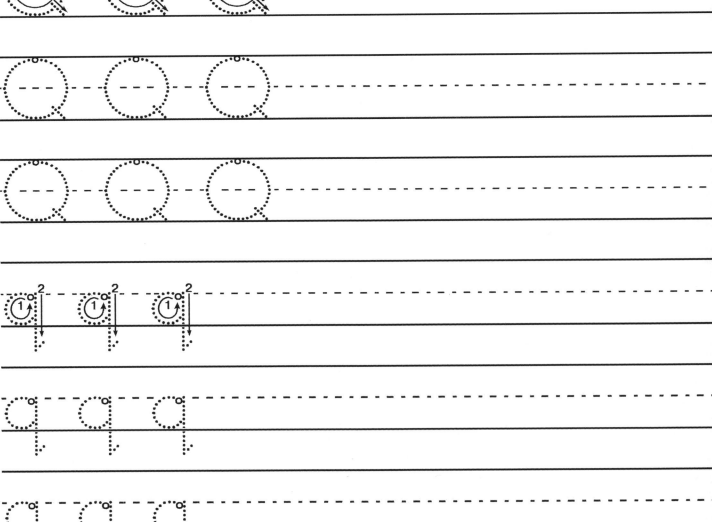

Quiet

Quetzal

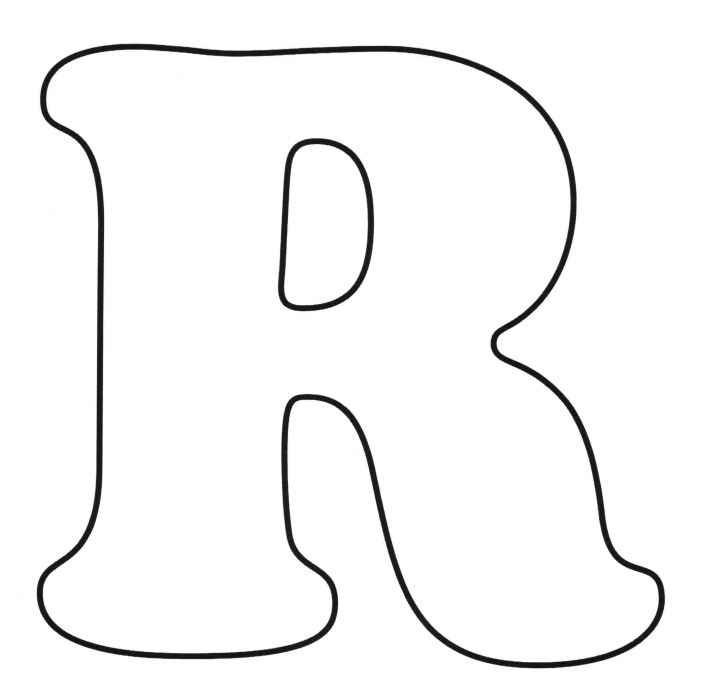

R R R

R R R

R R R

r r r

r r r

r r r

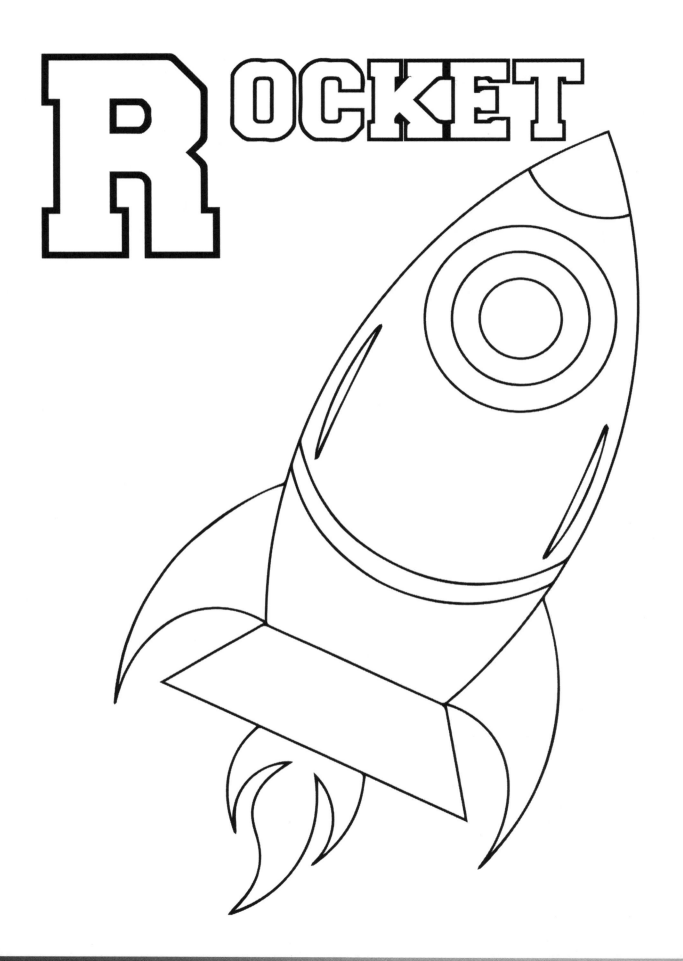

Rhino

Rabbit

R r

Ss   Sun

S S S

S S S

S S S

S S S

S S S

S S S

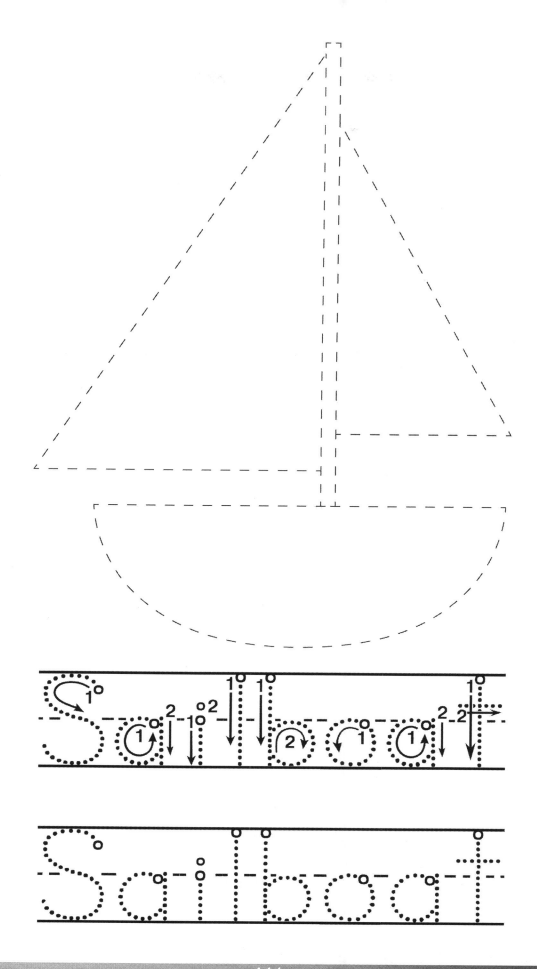

Sailboat

SEAHORSE

Snail

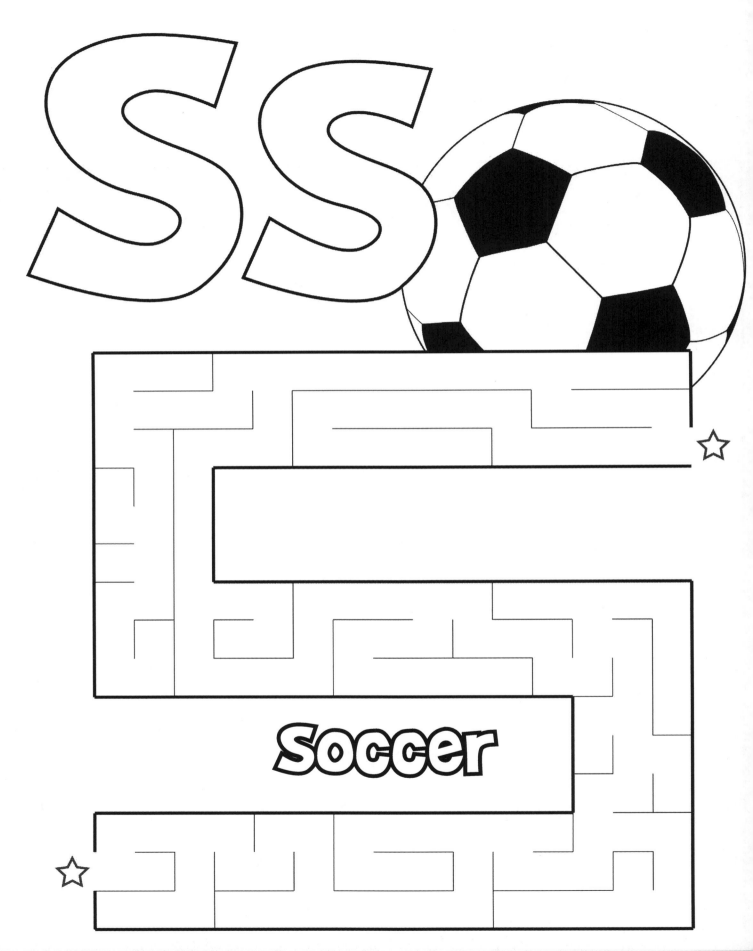

Soccer

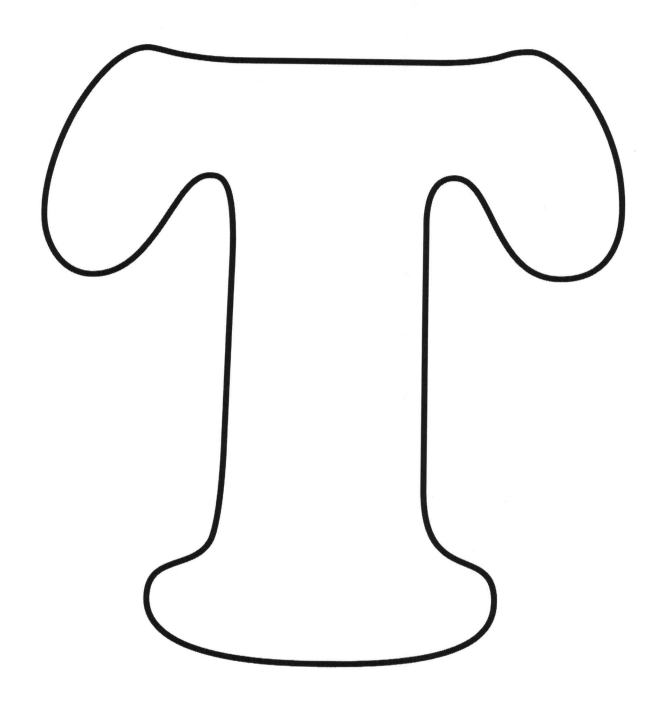

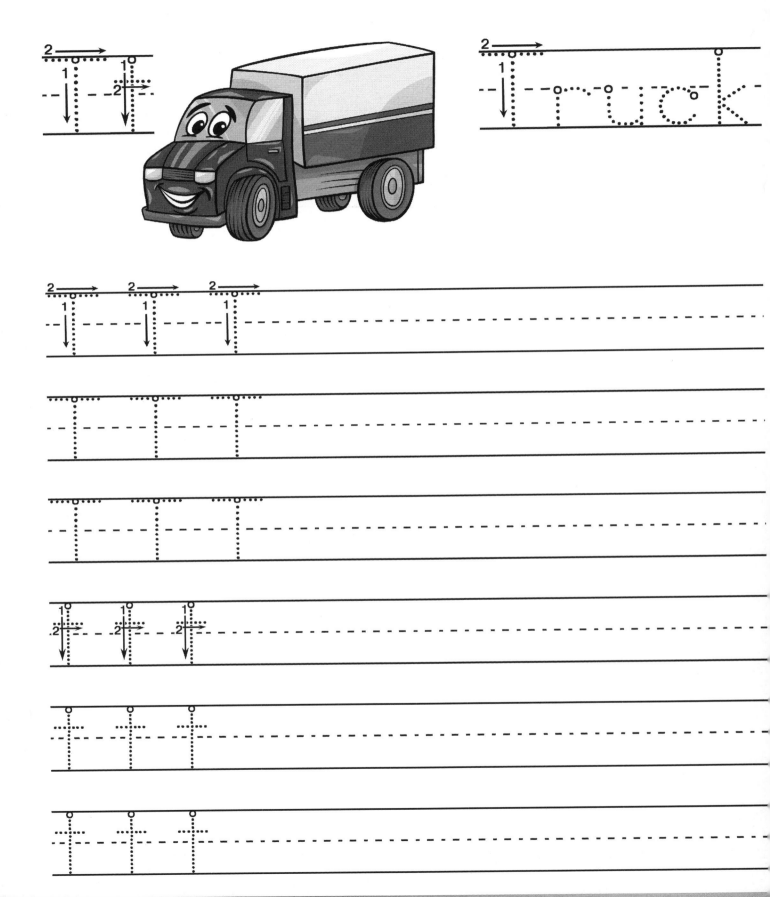

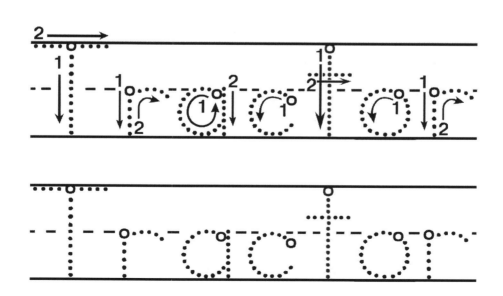

Turtle

Tambourine

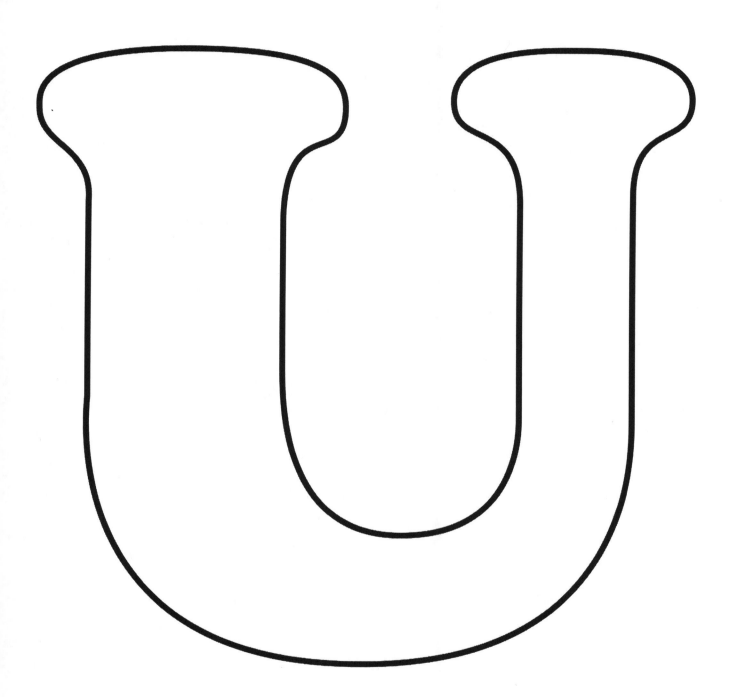

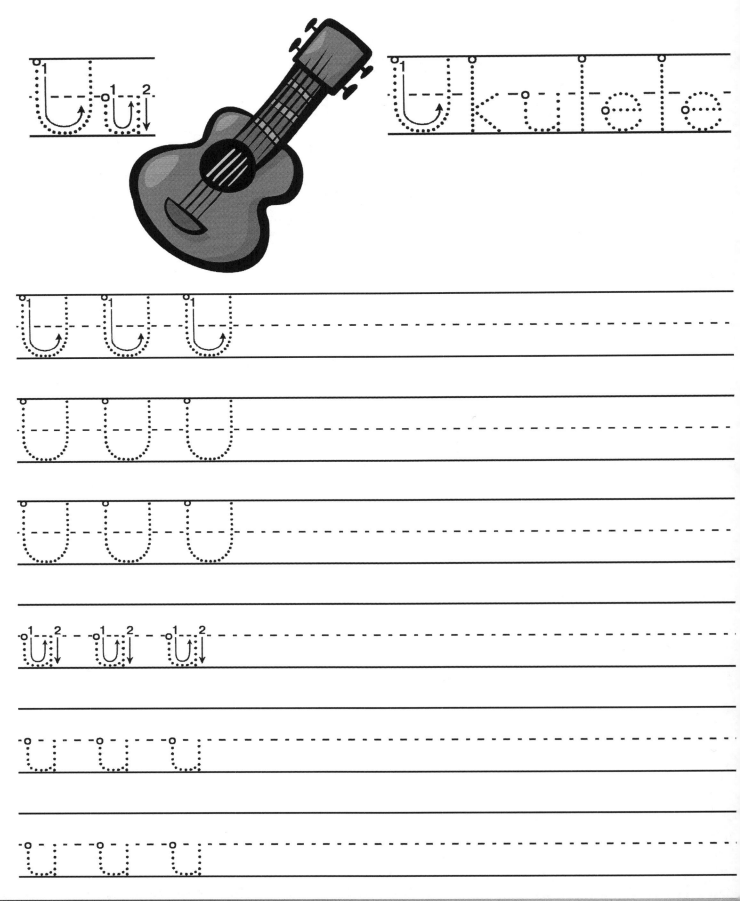

UMBRELLA

Underwater

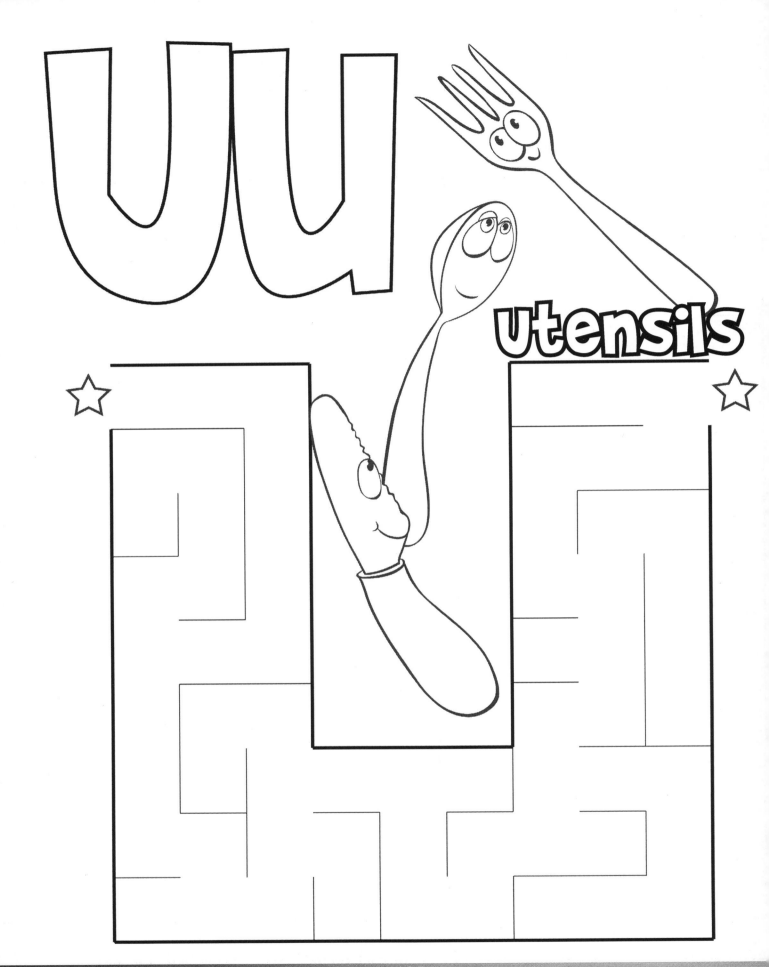

utensils

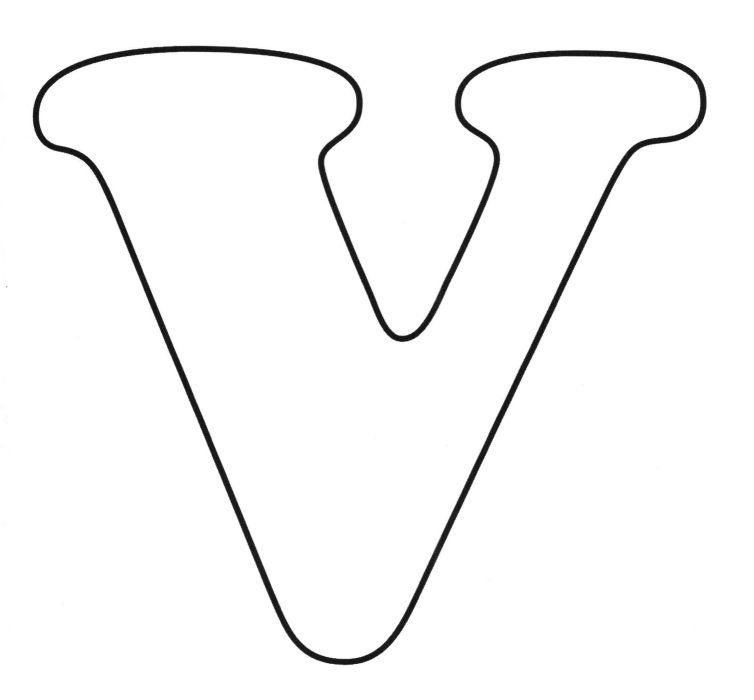

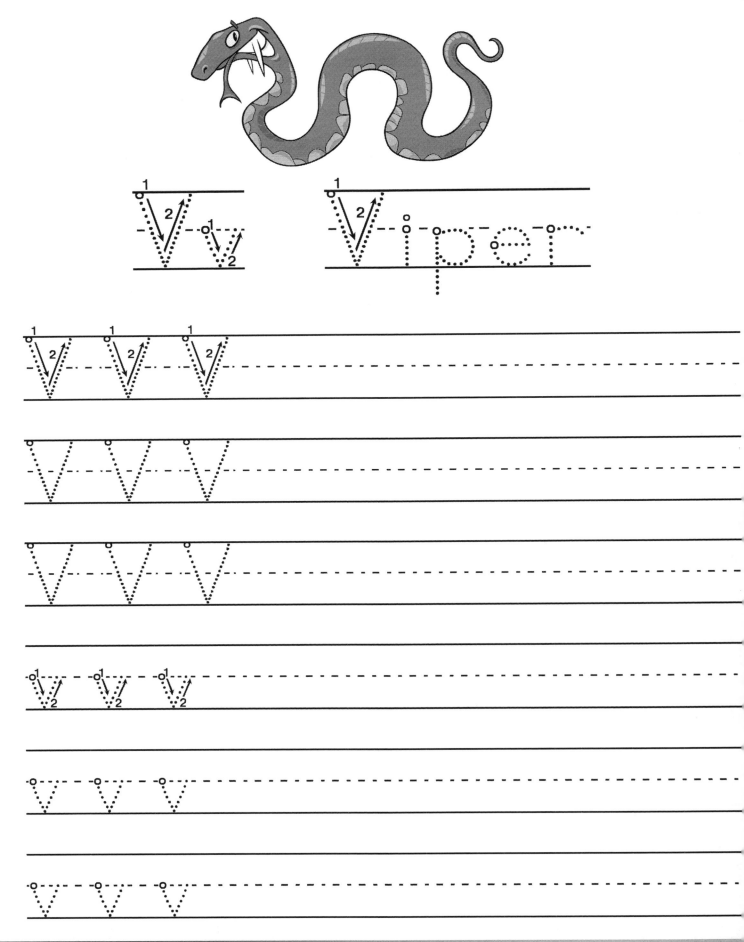

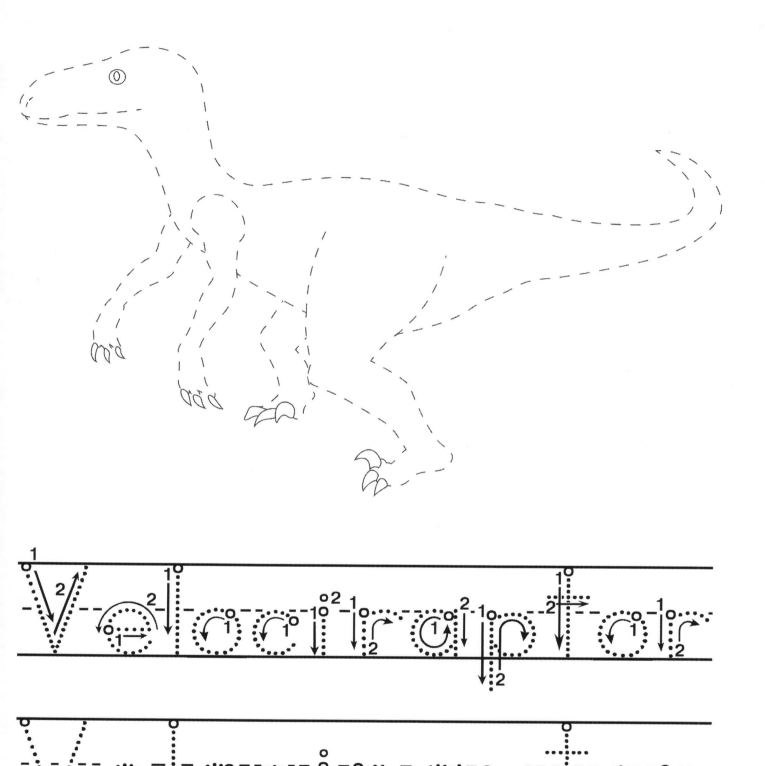

Vacation

Valentine

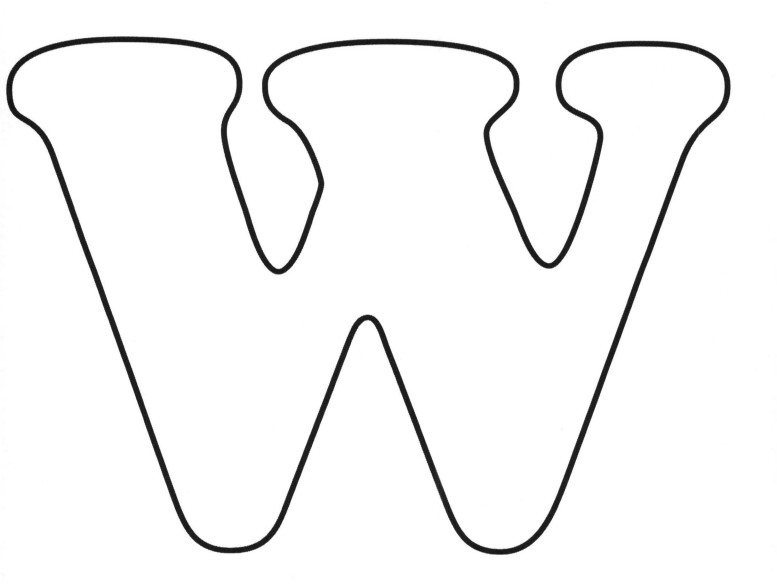

Weasel

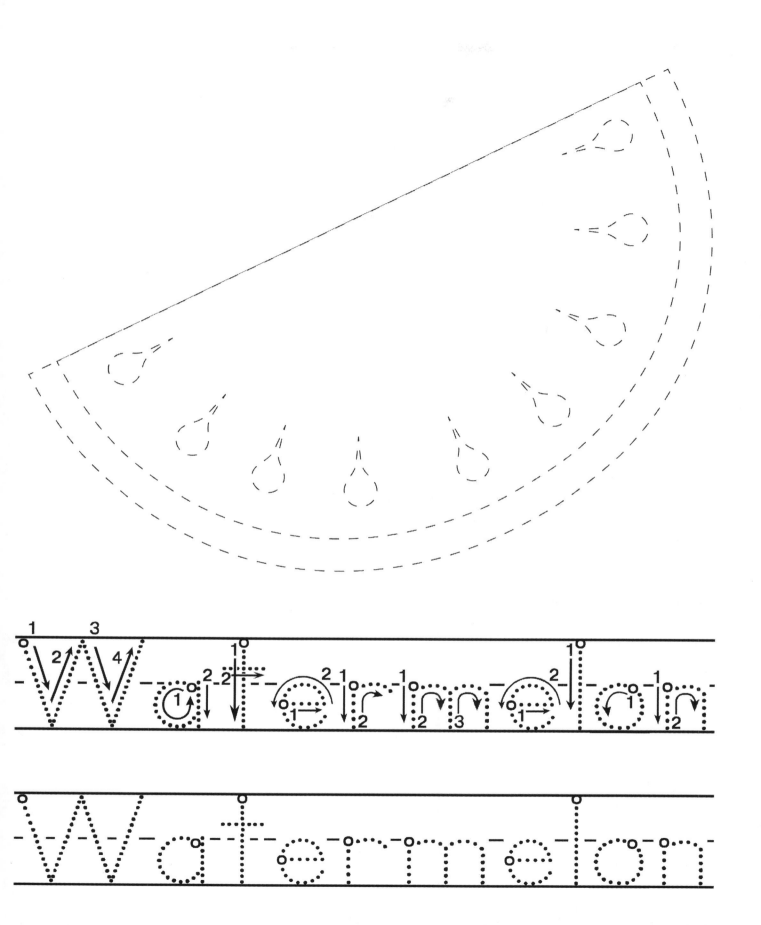

WALRUS

Whale

wreath

Xmas

X-RAY TETRA

xenops Bird

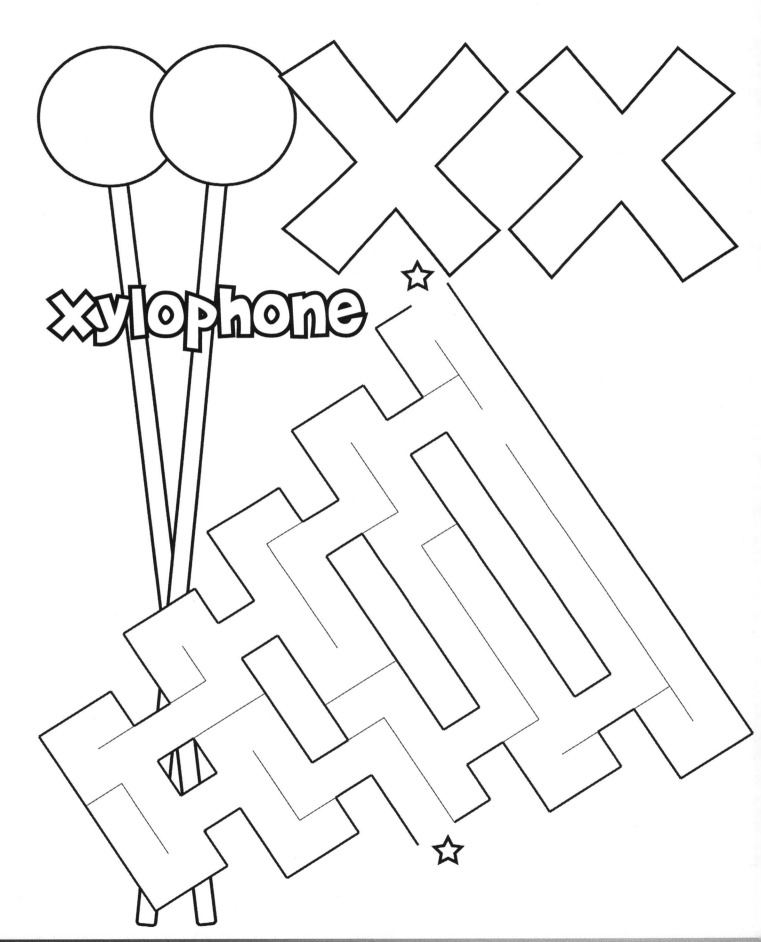

xylophone

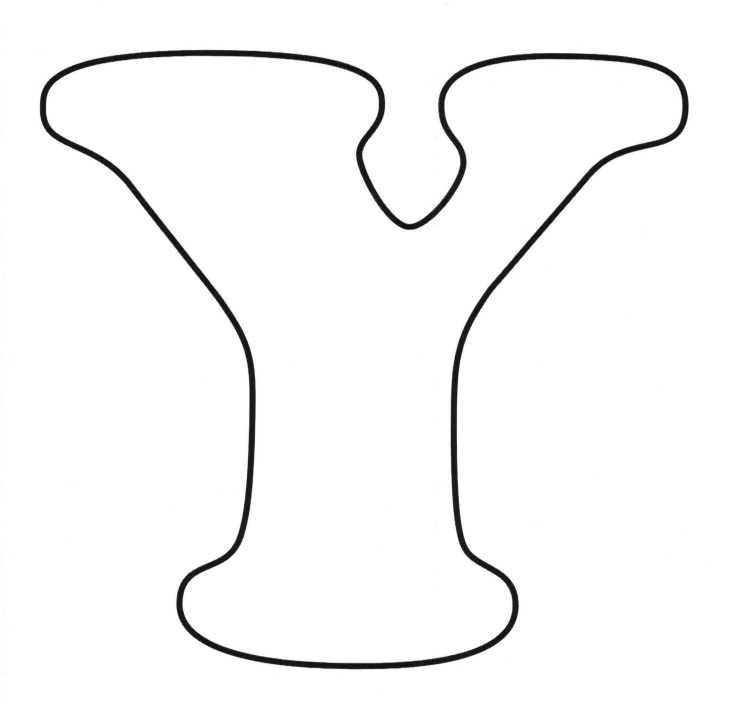

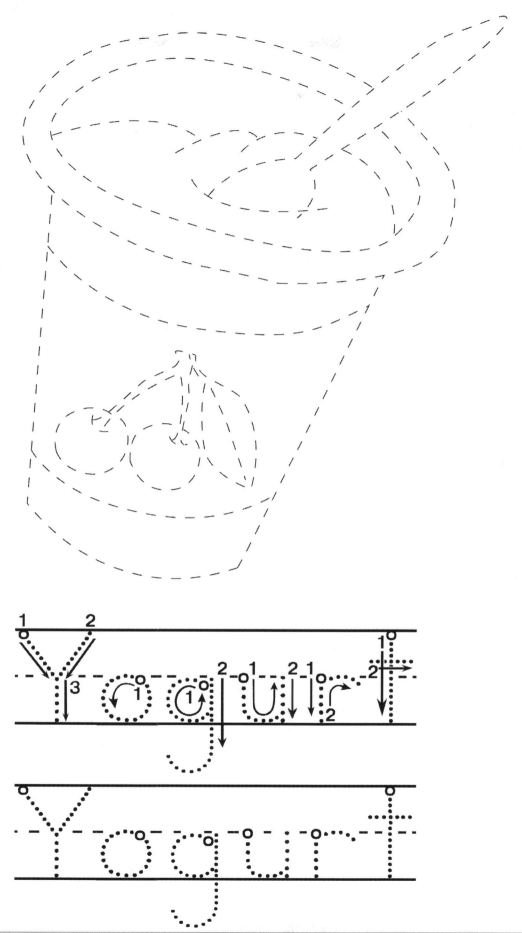

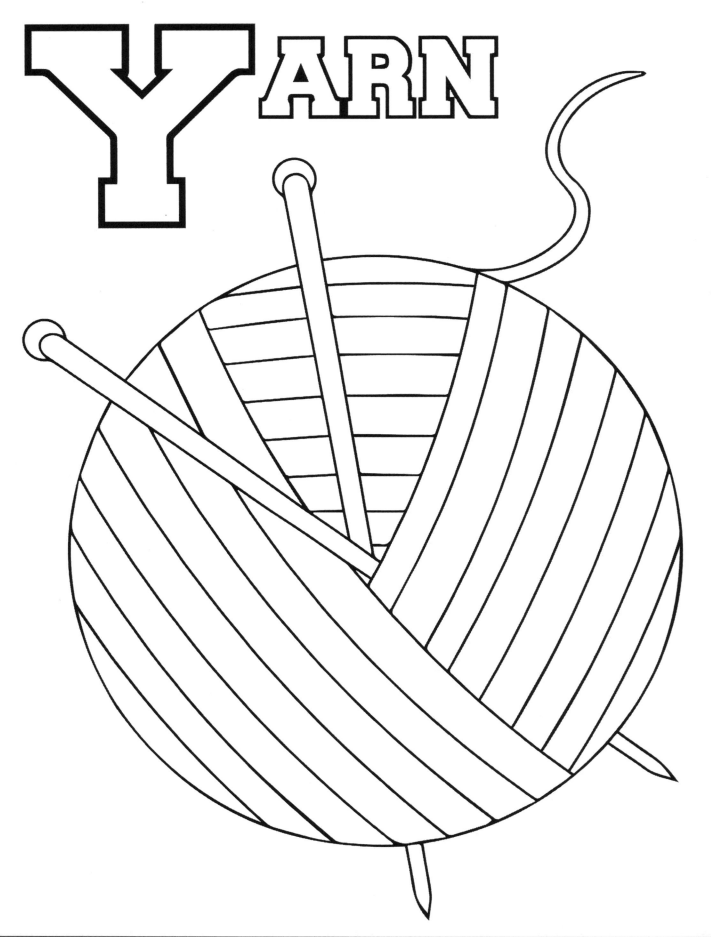

Yardwork

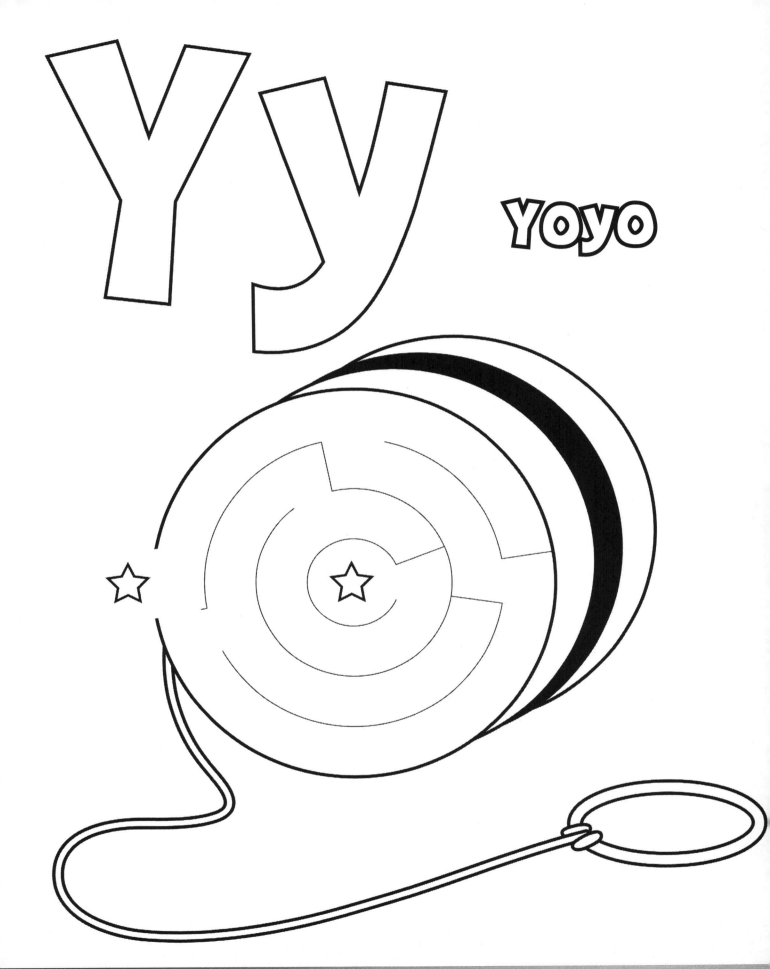

YoYo

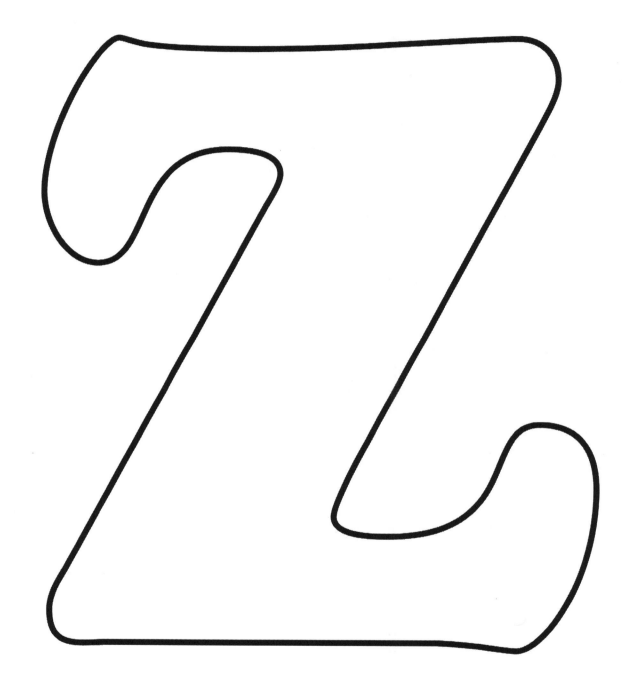

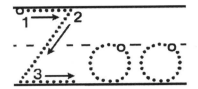

Zebra

ZIPPER

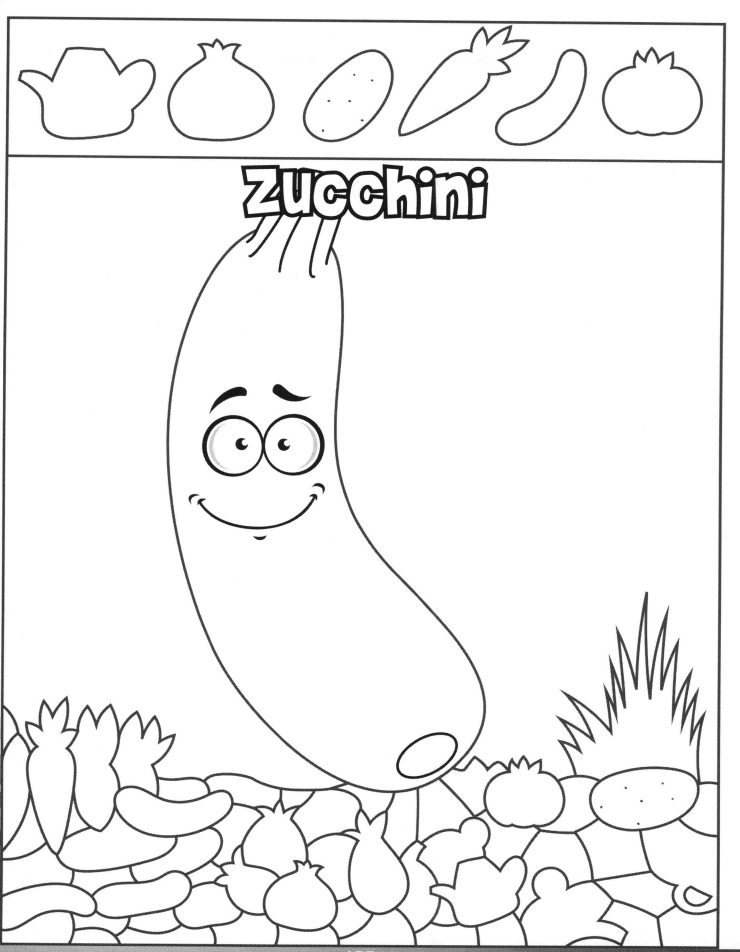

Zucchini

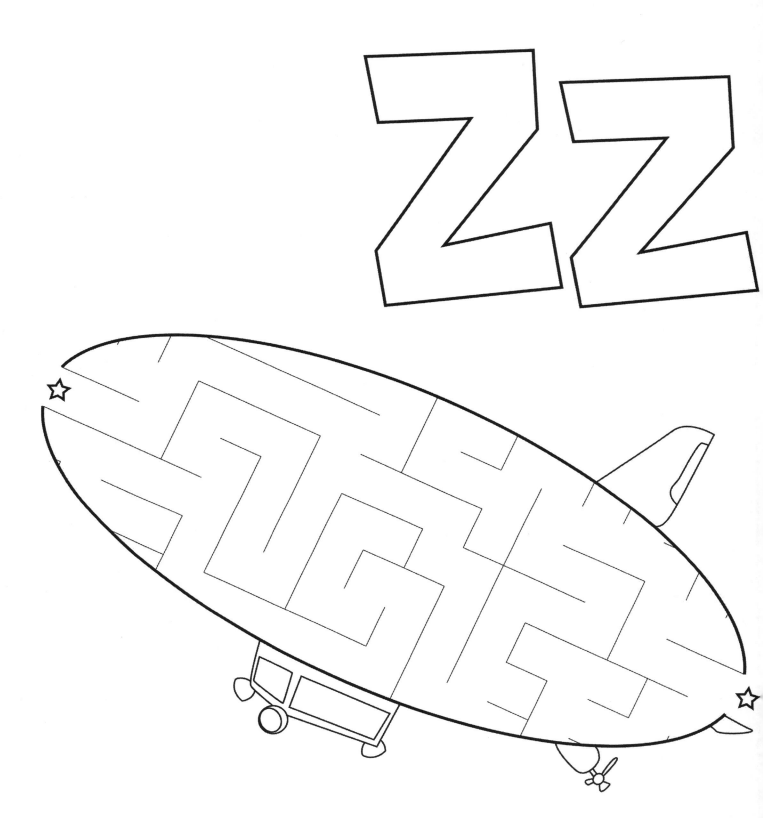

zeppelin

ABC

ALPHABET PRACTICE

A B C D E
F G H I J
K L M N
O P Q R
S T U V
W X Y Z

Alphabet Practice!

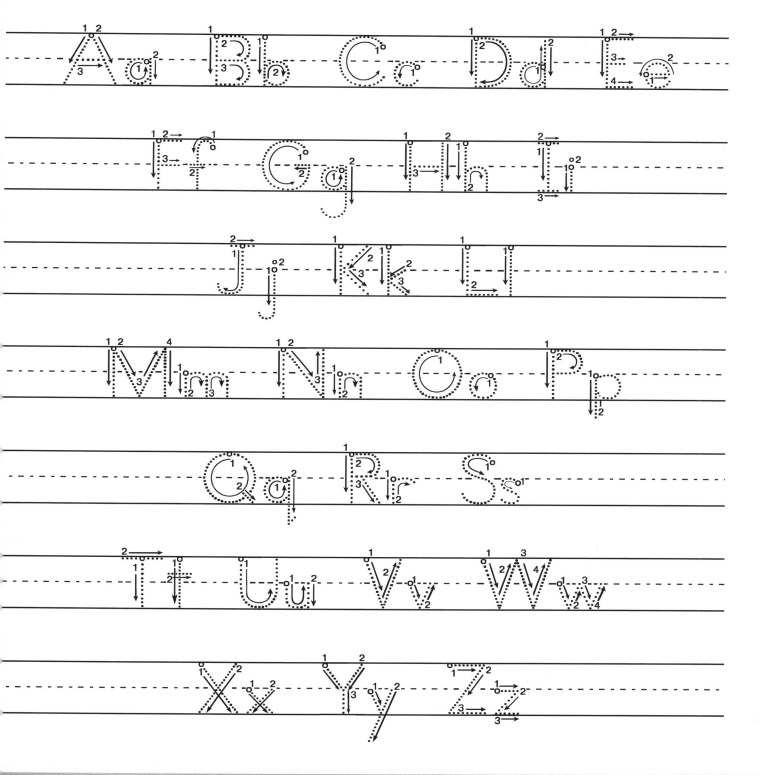

Lowercase Alphabet Practice!

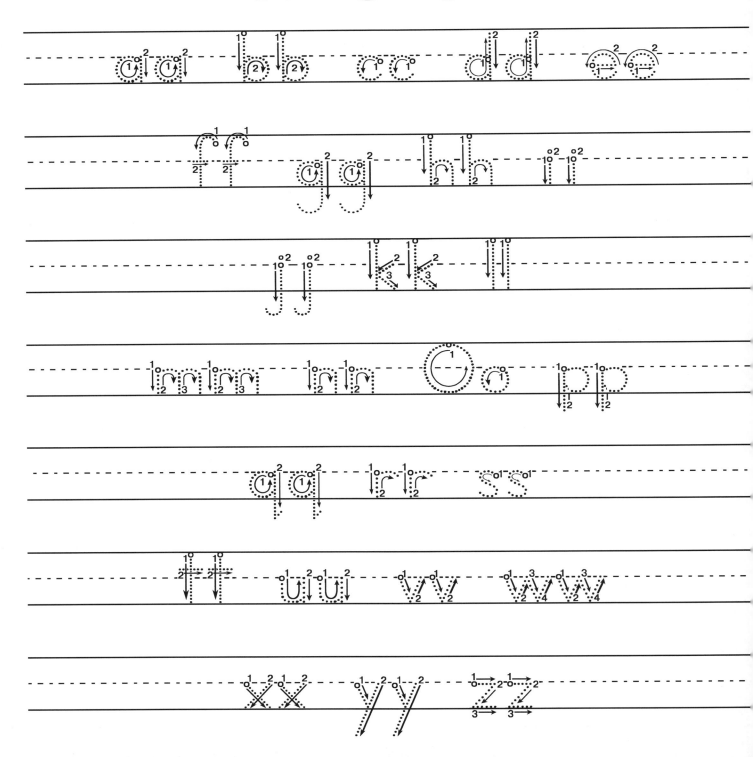

Uppercase Alphabet Practice!

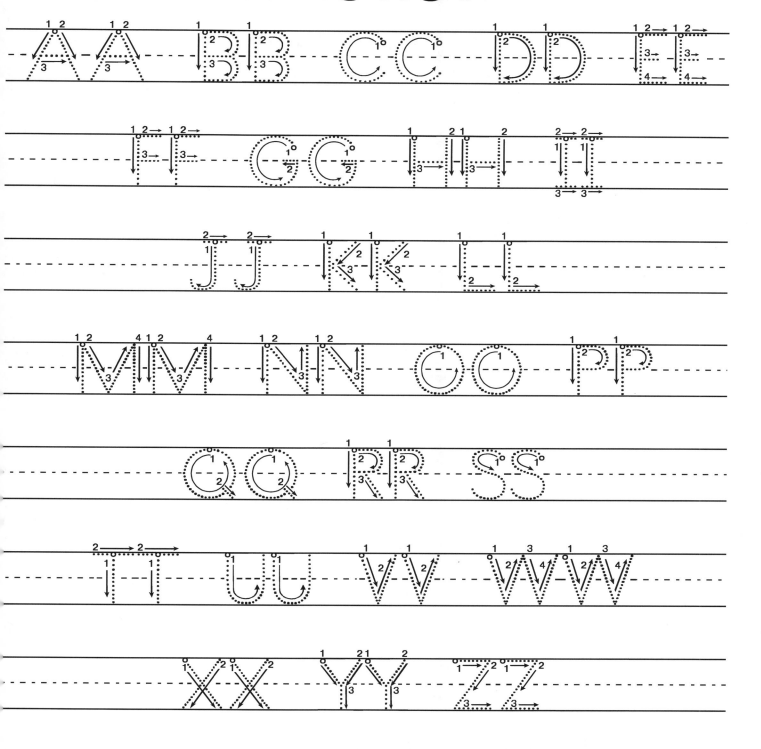

Fill in the Missing Letters!

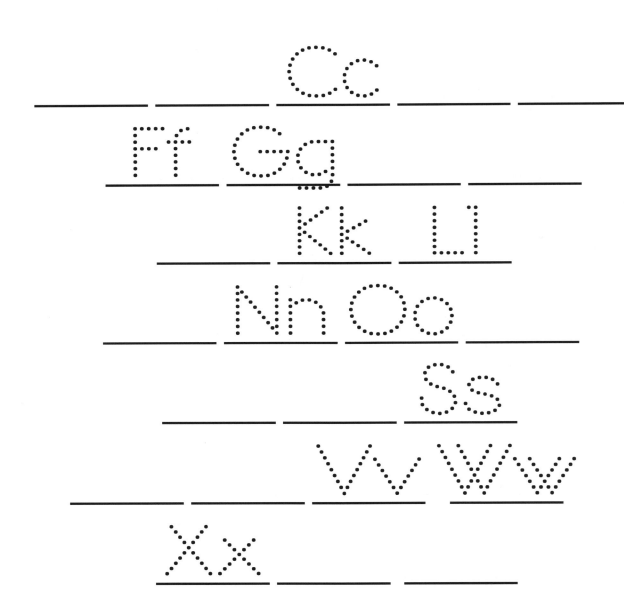

Cc

Ff Gg

Kk Ll

Nn Oo

Ss

Vv Ww

Xx

Fill in the Missing Letters!

Aa Bb __ __ Dd Ee

__ __ Hh Ii

Jj __ __

Mm __ __ Pp

Qq Rr __

Tt Uu __

__ Yy Zz

Fill in the First Letter!

_____ lien

_____ aby

_____ ake

_____ onut

_____ arth

_____ ox

_____ uitar

_____ eart

_____ guana

_____ anitor

_____ iwi

_____ eaf

_____ ouse

_____ urse

_____ nion

_____ ig

_____ uestion

_____ obot

_____ un

_____ ruck

_____ kulele

_____ easel

_____ iper

_____ mas

_____ ak

_____ oo

167

Free Download!

Like this book?

Join our VIP mailing list and get a _FREE_ 70 page printable PDF *Holiday Activity Book for Kids*! It includes crosswords, word searches, picture matching, and coloring activities for ages 4-10!

Holidays include:
  Martin Luther King Jr. Day
  Valentine's Day
  St. Patrick's Day
  Easter
  Earth Day
  4th of July
  Halloween
  Thanksgiving
  Hanukkah
  Christmas

Get Started here:

www.woojr.com/free-book

CERTIFICATE OF COMPLETION

This certificate confirms that

_____

(name here)

has completed all letter tracing, word tracing,
coloring pages, and mazes in the Alphabet Book for Kids,
a Woo! Jr. Kids book of ABC Activities, and Fun!

GREAT JOB!

Made in the USA
Las Vegas, NV
02 November 2020